FAITH

WORKS

FAITH

WORKS

R. Russell Bixler

Treasure House

An Imprint of

Destiny Image® Publishers, Inc.
P.O. Box 310
Shippensburg, PA 17257-0310

"For where your treasure is,
there will your heart be also." Matthew 6:21

ISBN 1-56043-338-8

For Worldwide Distribution
Printed in the U.S.A.

This book and all other Destiny Image, Revival Press,
and Treasure House books are available
at Christian bookstores and distributors worldwide.

For a U.S. bookstore nearest you, call **1-800-722-6774**.
For more information on foreign distributors,
call **717-532-3040**.
Or reach us on the Internet: **http://www.reapernet.com**

Contents

Foreword

I first met Russ and Norma Bixler when their children were students at Oral Roberts University. Over these many years, we have come into a wonderful relationship built on trust, friendship, and the healing power of God through the authority of Jesus' name.

This is the true life story of Christian pioneering faith, of hearing the voice of God about television, and of being obedient to His call. This story is living proof that no obstacle can stand in the way when believing God and hard work meet with the inspiration of the Holy Spirit.

I am proud to be associated with Cornerstone TeleVision and to be a co-laborer for souls with Russ and Norma.

—Richard Roberts
President and Chief Executive Officer
Oral Roberts University

Preface

As a young person, my family was one of the beneficiaries of Cornerstone TeleVision's ministry through a low-power station that originally picked up the signal from their Altoona station. At the time all I knew was that we could now watch some of the Christian programs that we never could before. Until I picked up this manuscript, however, I had no idea of the hard work, hot tears, and heartaches that went into a seemingly effortless broadcast on our little TV. Believe me, I now have a much deeper appreciation and respect for Russ and Norma Bixler and the ministry of Cornerstone TeleVision.

Russ Bixler's story of how Cornerstone TeleVision began will encourage every person into whose heart God has dropped an impossible dream. More than 20 years ago, Russ was a pastor who simply loved God and loved to minister to God's people. He had no intention of doing anything remotely connected with television. But then God interrupted the lives of the Bixlers with a divine mandate: Build a Christian television station. What followed is chronicled for you in these pages.

I think perhaps one of the most valuable lessons revealed in this history of Cornerstone TeleVision is, if God has told you to do something, then don't give up, no matter what the obstacle. The victory will come! Much as we would prefer an idyllic process, most of life just doesn't happen that way. We are actively working against an enemy force and must be prepared to hold on to our faith and press through. Cornerstone Tele-Vision did press on, and today its success—before both God and man—is a testimony to the power and grace of our Lord Jesus Christ.

Faith Works is the honest story of how God's working in one man's life can make a difference in the Kingdom. May the Lord stir your own heart as you read this inspiring book.

Jeanette M. Sprecher, Editor
Destiny Image Publishers

Chapter 1

"Not Me!"

In late August 1969, my wife Norma received a phone call from her friend Flo Dodge.

"How would you like to accompany me to the Christian Broadcasting Network in Virginia? I'm going to apply for a job at CBN."

"I don't think I can get away," Norma replied.

"It's only for three days."

"Well, if Russell agrees, I'll go."

Our daughter had just gone off to college, leaving Norma solely responsible for cooking for me and our three hungry boys. The possibility of leaving us to fend for ourselves seemed remote.

When she presented me with the idea, I quickly replied, "Sure. I think you *should* visit CBN."

"You do?" Norma responded, shocked by my positive answer.

I guess I even surprised myself.

Little did we know that this brief visit to CBN headquarters in Portsmouth, Virginia, would radically change our lives and point us in a completely different direction.

"**Y**ou're going to be on *The 700 Club* tonight," Flo told Norma as they surveyed the grounds where CBN's new building was located. "I'd better fix your hair."

"I'm not going to be on *The 700 Club*!" Norma objected.

"Yes, you are," Flo insisted—and she fixed Norma's hair.

Not yet syndicated across the nation, *The 700 Club* was seen on only one little CBN-owned station in Portsmouth, Virginia—Channel 27.

That evening Norma and Flo were seated in the viewing room above the studio, preparing to watch *The 700 Club*.

Suddenly, a young man whom they had met earlier in the day burst into the room.

"Norma, are you born again and filled with the Holy Spirit? And do you believe in healing?" he asked breathlessly.

Before she could answer, he said authoritatively, "If so, come with me."

Leaving Flo alone in the viewing room, Norma followed him downstairs to the studio where the telephone counselors were also seated.

"Sit there," he instructed, pointing to the first prayer phone, closest to *The 700 Club* set.

"Not Me!"

As the program began, Norma noticed that the show's host, Pat Robertson, was seated nearby. When the cameras focused on Pat, Norma could be seen in the background talking on the phone with viewers who called in for prayer.

Flo was right. Norma did indeed appear on television—and her hair looked great!

The next day, while Flo completed several projects for Pat Robertson, Norma waited in the CBN lobby.

CBN headquarters in August 1969, when Norma visited it.

Suddenly, the Spirit of God spoke to her. "I want you and Russell to build a station like this in Pittsburgh."

Norma protested, "But where will we get the money?"

3

That inner Voice responded, "The money's there."

"Where will we get the people?"

"The people you need are there. I will raise them up."

"Well, will anybody watch?"

"Yes, they will watch."

With every objection the Spirit of God assured her that He would take care of building the station.

Norma didn't mention the divine visitation to Flo on the long ride back to Pennsylvania. By the time she arrived home, Norma was about to burst.

When she bounced through the door of our parsonage, Norma was trembling with energy and excitement. I was happy to see her after our three-day separation, but I wasn't prepared for such a dramatic encounter.

With barely a wifely greeting, she nearly shouted, "Russell! The Lord said we're to build a Christian television station here in Pittsburgh!"

As I tried to give Norma the appropriate hug and kiss, she was bubbling over with excitement. "The Lord told me! He really spoke to me while I was at CBN!"

"That's a great idea—for Pat Robertson!" I snapped.

Why should I want a Christian TV station? As pastor of the Pittsburgh Church of the Brethren, my plate was already full and truly overflowing.

Two-and-a-half years earlier, Norma and I had been baptized in the Holy Spirit. Until then, I had been a shy, focused preacher, totally immersed in my little congregation.

"Not Me!"

In 1967, the Holy Spirit in His fullness had suddenly turned me outward: I saw the rest of the world in a new light. The Spirit of God had in a sense given me "X-ray vision," and I was now seeing beyond the four walls of the Pittsburgh Church of the Brethren. In fact, I was reaching out to people of other denominations—including Roman Catholics. Although I had long despised the Catholic Church, my heart suddenly overflowed with new love for my Catholic brothers and sisters in Christ.

When I visited the Duquesne University Outpouring with Harald Bredesen in early 1967 and saw dozens of young Catholics on fire for Jesus, God took my theology, turned it upside down, and dumped it out! I have loved the Roman Catholics ever since.

As one friend has said, "Russ Bixler got filled with the Holy Spirit and took off like a jet plane!"

Our tiny Church of the Brethren held 175 people comfortably, including the choir. I knew our pews' exact seating capacity because—until 1967—it was only full on Easter.

The week after we received the Holy Spirit, God spoke in my spirit, "Schedule a Sunday evening prayer service!"

Then, somehow, God began to draw 400-plus excited worshipers—most of them Roman Catholic—into our small church on Sunday evenings. People would squeeze into every little corner. We were experiencing what is usually called "revival."

For several years, I didn't even realize what was happening. Then an old-time Pentecostal preacher visited one Sunday and explained as he left, "That's exactly what we experienced in 1919!"

I had assumed it was normal Christianity—and perhaps it *was* what Jesus would consider normal Christianity. The Book of Acts was coming alive in my very life! Miracles were occurring by the dozens.

One Sunday, as I looked at all those people pouring in, even from out-of-state, I thought, *Wow! I'm really building a big church here!*

The Lord promptly spoke to my heart, "You can't have one of them! Send them back where they came from!"

So I did. Backslidden Presbyterians, Lutherans, Roman Catholics, and others returned to their churches on fire for Jesus. Many of them, however, discovered to their disappointment that their pastors didn't want fire—they just wanted peace.

As a result, when people mentioned Russ Bixler's name around Pittsburgh, they'd either get hugged—or slugged!

Some pastors, however, were earnestly seeking revival for themselves and their churches. God apparently saw their need and told me to organize a monthly meeting for pastors who had been filled with the Holy Spirit.

Soon traditional Pentecostal and mainline denominational pastors were attending in equal numbers and worshiping the Lord with growing fervency. These monthly luncheons became the catalyst that helped to ignite revival fires throughout the Greater Pittsburgh area.

Christians were flocking to any meeting where believers were worshiping Jesus and where the gifts of the Holy Spirit were in operation. New songs of praise from around the world spread like wildfire from one congregation to the other. People were devouring the Bible and hungrily seeking more and more teaching from God's Word.

During this time, the Spirit told me to have a conference, which we later named the Greater Pittsburgh Charismatic Conference. Thousands came to hear well-known Christian leaders from around the world teach and minister in the power of the Holy Spirit.

"Not Me!"

Organizing this annual conference—which didn't end until 20 years later, in 1987—required months of preparation. The Conference peaked in 1976, with attendees from 40 states and 15 nations.

At the same time, glorious miracles of salvation, deliverance, and healing were occurring repeatedly in my own ministry. A continuing flow of the supernatural had swept us up and continued to carry us forward.

I felt as if I were already on the ground floor of a divine avalanche, and now my wife wanted me to build a Christian television station!

Norma continued to bubble about how God had spoken to her about a Christian TV station in Pittsburgh.

I just looked at her with disdain and snarled, "I'm not interested!"

God had been pouring so many glorious experiences into my life that I was not looking for any more excitement. After all, I was a pastor whose ministry was exploding with great and wonderful miracles.

Norma began to argue with me, but I refused even to consider what she was suggesting.

"Well, if God wants me to do it," I finally exclaimed, "He can tell *me*!"

I was not going to take on a new venture just because Norma said so. Besides, I didn't know anything about television and really wasn't interested in it.

Norma began using her feminine wiles—and nobody knows how to turn on the feminine charm better than Norma. When that didn't work, she became angry and abusive. She tried other angles, but nothing succeeded.

Finally, after about two weeks of pleading, Norma gave up and said, "All right, Holy Spirit, You told me; now *You* tell him!"

That's exactly what the Spirit of God had been waiting for. When Norma stopped talking and started praying, the Holy Spirit went to work.

Over the next several months, I began to have an uncomfortable sensation in my spirit about this whole matter. Norma didn't talk to me about television any more, but she did talk to other people. Some Christians started getting excited about it.

In December of that year—1969—a pastor-friend, John Zerby, contacted me. I was upstairs in the parsonage when the phone rang, so I walked into the bedroom to answer it.

"Brother Russ, what's God doing about a Christian television station?" he asked.

"I don't know, and I don't care!" I answered.

John ignored me: "Well, I feel God wants a Christian television station."

"I'm not interested."

"I think we should place a fleece before the Lord," he suggested, undaunted.

"I hate fleeces!"

John continued to ignore me. "I think we should say....Let's just place this fleece before the Lord: If You want a Christian television station in Pittsburgh, then You have Pat Robertson do all the preliminary work on it."

With that, something happened inside me. The only way I can describe it is that the Holy Spirit turned cartwheels inside me—within my spirit.

I fell over on the bed.

I was astonished! I'd never had that experience before—and only once since.

I shouted, "John! The Lord is accepting that fleece!"

But John wasn't surprised at all.

I began to wonder, "What is this?"

It had already been about four months since Norma had returned from CBN saying that we were supposed to start a Christian television station.

The following Sunday evening at our church, Norma began to cry during the prayer service. Everyone looked at her, and she blubbered, "The Lord just said that He's giving us a Christian television station for Christmas!"

Then we all *really* stared at her. It was an awkward moment.

A Presbyterian who often visited the Sunday evening services had brought a businessman-friend to the service because he needed a miracle in his business (which he soon received). Later, as the two men left the church, the businessman said with a bit of a chuckle, "That nice lady thinks God's going to give her a television station!"

Today when Norma and I recall that incident, *we* chuckle.

The following March we drove to Georgia to attend a conference. On the trip south, Norma begged me to take her by way of the Christian Broadcasting Network in Virginia.

"That's out of the way," I argued.

Norma responded insistently, "We need to go by CBN!"

"Why?" I asked.

Norma reminded me of an incident that had happened three years earlier on the evening Jesus baptized both of us in the Holy Spirit.

We had been invited to a Full Gospel Businessmen's Fellowship Banquet, and Pat Robertson had made a special trip from Virginia to attend. After being introduced to the audience Pat exclaimed, "Let's all praise the Lord!" Instantly 800 pairs of hands shot into the air, and the praises were almost deafening. I sat there, confused and curious—I'd never heard such a chorus of worship.

I have no recollection of anything else Pat said that evening in 1967, but Norma remembered it all. Pat had added, "There's a Channel 40 available in the Pittsburgh area for a Christian television station, and someone in this meeting is supposed to build it."

Norma never forgot that statement.

"Don't you remember what Pat Robertson said about television that evening in 1967?"

"No," I replied honestly. I couldn't recall a word of it.

Thus she persisted: "We need to go by CBN!"

I thought about the matter of the fleece, which had gotten under my skin. "Okay," I agreed.

As we pulled into the parking lot at CBN, a car was parking right in front of us.

"That's him! That's him!" Norma shouted excitedly. "That's Pat Robertson!"

"Not Me!"

I got out and introduced myself.

Pat said, "Pittsburgh, huh? Pittsburgh....Come with me."

As we entered the station together, he told his secretary, "Cancel all my appointments for this afternoon."

After leading us into his office, Pat sat down and announced abruptly, "God said there's to be a Christian television station in Pittsburgh. You're the one who's supposed to build it."

"Not me!" I argued and used every lame excuse I could think of.

Norma was getting angrier by the minute, but she sat there quietly.

Pat, too, finally got disgusted with me. Abruptly he wheeled around in his swivel chair and pulled open a file drawer. As he lifted out a huge manila folder—about three inches thick—I could see over his shoulder in great big letters the word *Pittsburgh*. Inside were maps and surveys and all kinds of preliminary information and correspondence that Pat Robertson had done on his own.

I knew I was a "dead duck."

Norma saw it, too. She put her hands on her hips and just glared at me with that "now-will-you-believe-it?" look on her face.

I knew we had to build a Christian television station in Pittsburgh. God had planned that fleece just for me.

Pat needed only one little crack in the door from me, and he came rushing through.

11

"There's a Channel 40 available in your area," he said and started writing on several pieces of paper, which he later gave to me. "This is everything you'll need to do to get this project started."

Russ on *The 700 Club* with John Gilman, 1971.

Pat made a call to his Washington attorney and told him about me, saying, "Russ will be getting in touch with you."

Suddenly I started getting excited about the TV project. Pat operated with such forcefulness and speed that he actually had me visualizing the completed station.

He concluded the afternoon by saying, "I'd like you to spend the night with us, but our old farmhouse is being remodeled."

A CBN volunteer, Lucille Thompson, asked if we would like to stay at her apartment. Lucille, who was retired from the United States Navy, had been delightedly serving as Pat's volunteer secretary. A most gracious hostess, she sensed in her spirit that something of historic significance was occurring.

"Not Me!"

Now in her 80's, Lucille still rejoices with us from the Naval retirement home in Mississippi.

The next morning Pat came to her apartment to pray with us and to tie up some loose ends. We left Virginia with an intimidating list of projects to be accomplished in order to get the television station rolling.

Norma and I continued on our way to Georgia excited. In fact, we were soaring.

Returning to Pittsburgh from the conference a few days later, on Interstate 85 north of Charlotte, I said out loud, "Lord, I know You told both of us that we're supposed to build a Christian television station in Pittsburgh, but I'm scared. I don't know anything about television. I'm like Gideon, Lord. Could You give us another sign?"

Instantly Norma said, "Why, the Lord says 'Isaiah 49:22.' What does that say?"

"I don't know. There's the Bible on the seat between us. Look it up."

While we were driving along Norma read:

*Thus says the Lord God: "Behold, I will lift up My hand to the nations, and **raise my signal** to the peoples...."*

The atmosphere in the car was absolutely electric for the next five or ten miles! We sat there in awe. I didn't know there was a television scripture in the Bible!

That one word from God kept us going for the next nine years. We were to experience absolute horror stories. Before the station was completed, we went through "hell on earth."

I've often said that building a Christian television station is "a modern form of crucifixion." And I still believe it. We were

13

to need the scriptural assurance of Isaiah 49:22 again and again.

P at Robertson had told us that we needed about $3,000 to cover initial legal fees and other miscellaneous expenses.

After returning home, Norma and I asked a friend to donate $3,000 for the project, which she graciously provided.

God was setting everything in motion.

To get the ball rolling, I called a group of about 30 pastors and businessmen together for a meeting in our church. Pat Robertson came from Virginia and encouraged us to be persistent during the months ahead.

That evening Pat made a very knowledgeable statement to the group: "Building a Christian television station is like walking into the teeth of a blizzard. The wind and snow make walking quite difficult, but it cannot stop you. Only *you* can stop you! You must keep walking."

Pat spent the night in our home. When Norma shared with him the vision God had given her, Pat was fascinated by the fact that the vision had occurred at CBN some months before.

As we reminisced, Norma and I remembered that we had received the Holy Spirit in 1967, and Pat had been present at that very service. Indeed, Pat Robertson has been involved in our lives at several crucial moments.

In an effort to do everything properly, we promptly formed a nonprofit corporation. Attorney Ross Thompson was on our first Board of Directors, and he put together the Articles of Incorporation and the initial by-laws. He filed those papers with the Commonwealth of Pennsylvania; he also filed for nonprofit status 501(c)(3) with the Internal Revenue Service.

We began to speak publicly about the project of a Christian television station. I was so excited that I assumed every other Spirit-filled Christian would be excited, too.

Earlier I had told Pat Robertson that many churches in Pittsburgh would get behind it, but he warned me solemnly, "Not only will they *not* support you, but many of the pastors will actively resist you!"

"Pittsburgh is different," I had assured Pat. "We're in the midst of a great move of God, and pastors are joining together in cooperative efforts."

Pat simply shook his head.

I knew nothing about what I was doing except that God had said to do it—and I thought that was all I needed to know.

Surely everyone would be thrilled about starting a Christian television station. After all, God had wonderfully blessed every project He had instructed me to accomplish for the Kingdom.

What a shock it was to find not only a number of my pastor-friends indifferent, but also a few who were actually quite hostile.

"But God specifically told me to build a Christian TV station!" I would protest.

They would shrug their shoulders or perhaps offer some silly excuse.

Slowly I began to realize that the typical pastor, instead of being excited about a great new tool for expanding the Kingdom of God, perceived that the television station might divert money from his church.

(Actually, a subsequent nationwide scientific survey by the University of Pennsylvania revealed to everyone's surprise that the people who give the most money to Christian television ministries also give the most to their own local churches. To this day, few pastors believe that survey.)

But some ministers—and a lot of laymen—*were* interested. Still, it became apparent that we faced an uphill battle.

Michael Harper, formerly an Anglican priest, was speaking that year at the Greater Pittsburgh Charismatic Conference. Norma felt that she needed prayer to stand firm on the TV project and asked Michael to pray for her, although she did not specifically mention television.

Michael prayed briefly, then suddenly stopped and stared at Norma. "The Lord says, 'Behold, I have set before you an open door, which no one is able to shut'" (Revelation 3:8a).

Norma kept that prophetic word of assurance in her heart for many years.

When Norma was saved—on Ash Wednesday of 1967—at the age of 38, she had two expected responses. First was, "Why did I wait so long?"

The second response came one day while she was shopping in downtown Pittsburgh. The Spirit of God showed her the emptiness in the eyes of the people passing on the sidewalk.

"Oh Lord, how can I tell all these troubled people about You?" Norma asked.

The Spirit of God had obviously heard that prayer and given her the vision for reaching those empty lives—through television.

Chapter 2

Into the Teeth of the Blizzard

"The Federal Communications Commission has closed the door on any new applications for Channel 40," our Washington attorney informed me over the phone.

"What?" I could not believe the shocking news. Someone else would get the Construction Permit!

"Lord! How can we build a TV station without a channel?"

To prevent signal interference, the FCC limits the number of channels that can be used for broadcasting in a city. With the Pittsburgh area's one remaining television allocation suddenly beyond our reach, we had run out of options.

We had already announced a prayer meeting to be held at Beulah Presbyterian Church, a congregation with a number of Spirit-filled members.

With sadness in my voice, I announced to about 50 precious souls that we couldn't build a station without a channel allocation. Then we went into a period of prayer.

Suddenly we were startled to hear a loud, stentorian, male voice proclaim, "This television station is of Me, and I will build it! You are to begin contributing money *now!*"

It was Ray Wenger, one of a number of quiet Mennonites from Scottdale, Pennsylvania. The shyest of the quiet people, Ray seldom opened his mouth. In fact, few people actually knew what his voice sounded like.

We all stared at Ray, who was flushed with embarrassment and astonished at himself. He looked like the boy caught with his hand in the cookie jar.

One thing we all knew—that word had to be from God.

"I never did anything like that in my life!" Ray muttered. It was his one and only prophetic word.

That evening we began accepting monthly pledges—a number of them from Christians who would not have pledged if God hadn't nudged Ray Wenger. And there wasn't even a channel available!

We called the monthly pledges "The Three Thousand Club," named for the 3,000 who were added to the Church at Pentecost.

God had already instructed me to organize a "120 Club"— the number of Christians who pioneered the Church at Pentecost. Supporters could pledge to purchase a certificate of deposit as collateral for future loans to the Western Pennsylvania Christian Broadcasting Company.

Although many people had pledged to give, we hadn't yet made serious requests for cash contributions. I was feeling uneasy about accepting these contributions, reminding myself that I was receiving gifts for a channel that didn't even exist.

Into the Teeth of the Blizzard

Yet Christians began investing in a vision they could see only with the eyes of faith. They knew that God would pull it off somehow.

All of us were volunteers, excited about the prospect of a Christian television station. To detail our progress, I sent out a regular newsletter called *Good News for Western Pennsylvania*. It wasn't very professional, but it fulfilled the need for news—or *lack* of news.

At times our home would be packed with piles of newsletters and elbow-to-elbow volunteers. Occasionally we used our church or the South Park Baptist Church (located, of course, on Baptist Road) for the mailings. From the beginning, many

**Volunteers prepare the newsletter
mailing, 1972.**

gracious people were involved and put their faith to work in tangible ways.

Helen Mierski typed the newsletter and began keeping financial records in shoe boxes until we were able to get an accountant! Helen lovingly volunteered hundreds of hours and later became one of our valued employees at Cornerstone TeleVision—until her recent retirement.

I had a Christian friend who was a vice president of one of Pittsburgh's larger banks. After being turned down without serious consideration by the two largest banks, this vice president agreed to work with us.

Suddenly I found myself putting together financial statements and *pro formas*—documents quite unfamiliar to me.

At the same time, I was uneasy about the bank's representative who had been assigned to evaluate our project. He was not a Christian, nor was he the least bit sympathetic. When I tried gently to use the vice president's name, he reminded me, "This is my project, and I will decide if the bank will accept you!"

I found his attitude quite intimidating.

When at last the bank executive finished his investigation, I was called to meet with him again. He proceeded to "assault" me with facts and figures, few of which helped our cause.

"I made a number of phone calls across the nation to other banks and TV stations. The responses I received about your situation were quite pessimistic," he noted bluntly.

I prepared myself for the worst.

When he finished heaping all this negativism upon me, the executive frowned severely. "This will require a lot of work, but if you work hard and don't give up, you just might make it....In fact," he grinned, after an interminable pause, "I almost made a pledge myself!"

Ultimately he did make that contribution.

That's the way the nine-year roller coaster went—up one week and down the next week. We began to realize that when you invade the domain of "the prince of the power of the air" (Ephesians 2:2), there will ensue a horrendous warfare. Yet God is greater, and we were to build in that confidence. "He who is in you is greater than he who is in the world" (1 John 4:4b).

I felt a bit like the little boy who was going door to door, selling picture postcards for ten cents each.

"What are you going to do with the money?" he was asked.

"Oh, I'm raising a million dollars to support foreign missionaries."

"A million dollars! Do you expect to raise that much all by yourself?"

"Oh, no," the youngster answered. "Another boy is helping me."

S ince UHF television was not yet financially viable, the owners of the Construction Permit for Channel 22 turned their Permit back to the FCC within that year.

"Now there's a channel we can apply for!" I said when I learned of the news.

Before we could even assemble an application for Channel 22, the owners of the Permit for Channel 40 also returned their Permit.

One day we had no available channel, and suddenly there were two!

Pittsburgh's Channel 53 was also in trouble and went "dark" after losing millions of dollars.

With that news I immediately phoned Pat Robertson. "Channel 53 already has a station built and is waiting for a buyer!"

"I'll fly to Pittsburgh as soon as possible!" he replied eagerly.

In the meantime, I arranged a meeting for Pat, our lawyer, and the lawyer for the bankrupt company.

Pat negotiated hard on our behalf and worked out a tentative arrangement for a bargain purchase price of about a million dollars.

"We won't even have to build!" we exclaimed joyfully to one another. "The station is already sitting there!"

Then we experienced the first of many devastating turns of events that would dog us for nearly ten years.

Our attorney, who was quite familiar with bankruptcies, promptly went to the courthouse and inexplicably forced Channel 53 into "involuntary" bankruptcy. The attorney for the owners was infuriated—and for good reason.

Pat Robertson, who is also an attorney, was thoroughly disgusted, and he started to distance himself from us. At the time, however, I didn't realize that a change had begun to take place.

In the meantime, a well-heeled buyer showed up and purchased Channel 53.

This left us with the next course of action: To apply for Channel 22—a station allocation that had never been constructed.

Into the Teeth of the Blizzard

In spite of this setback, a faithful group of people continued to contribute toward the Christian television project.

Every Monday morning that summer I put together a bank deposit of the five- and ten-dollar contributions that people had given to me on Sunday. Then I would send our 14-year-old son Paul (who now works for Cornerstone TeleVision) to the bank on his bicycle.

"My dad is going to build a Christian TV station with that money," Paul would explain to the bank tellers.

The ladies thought he was cute but very naive.

No wonder. Five or ten dollars at a time doesn't build a multi-million dollar installation. We needed an "angel" who would use his estate as collateral for a large loan.

During one of our Sunday evening praise services, I mentioned this need to the congregation: "The television project is stalled for lack of money. But it could be done by using someone's assets as collateral."

After the service a medical doctor from out of town talked to Norma and said, "Here's my phone number. Have Russ call me tomorrow."

The doctor had brought his wife to Pittsburgh for a holiday weekend as a birthday gift. They had attended a show and done some sightseeing.

Then the doctor had asked his wife, "What would you like to do on Sunday evening?"

"Attend Russ Bixler's church!" was her immediate reply.

The only time I mentioned that particular need to the congregation was the very evening this couple attended our church—and God spoke to the doctor's heart in that moment.

This man provided hundreds of thousands of dollars in bonds as collateral for a construction loan.

Once again I was riding high—but not for long.

Our Washington attorney phoned with bad news: "A TV station in Baltimore has also filed for Channel 22 in Pittsburgh."

My hopes tumbled again.

"But we have an advantage," the attorney reminded me. "The Federal Communications Commission will always select the applicant who has no other broadcast interests—all other conditions being equal."

After some expensive legal maneuvering on our part, Julian Smith (founder of the company now known as Sinclair Broadcasting) agreed to let us keep Channel 22.

"There is one condition, however," our attorney warned us. "You must purchase all the major pieces of broadcast equipment within 18 months. If you don't have all that equipment on-site within the allotted time, you must forfeit the Construction Permit for Channel 22."

Although Julian Smith preferred the more desirable Channel 22, he applied for Channel 40.

We enjoyed a brief respite.

With the channel crisis averted, we excitedly prepared to bring Christian television to Pittsburgh.

From the beginning, Pat Robertson had enthusiastically agreed with me that *The 700 Club* would be carried on our Pittsburgh station after we went on the air. In the meantime, he decided to syndicate his program across the country and began to purchase air time on secular stations for *The 700 Club*.

I encouraged Pat in this work. "Pittsburgh will be your best market in the whole nation," I told him. "In fact, you will have more salvations, more contributions, more mail responses from here than from any other city."

Then I added, "Seattle will be your second-best city."

Just as I promised, Pittsburgh and Scattlc were *The 700 Club's* most responsive cities for the first several years.

Eager to have *The 700 Club* air in our area, I made all the preliminary arrangements for the program to be carried on Channel 53 in Pittsburgh. I found a Pittsburgh coordinator for CBN from our congregation, publicized the need for *The 700 Club* prayer partners, and helped to organize Pat's first telethon on Channel 53. I went on camera during the telethon and enthusiastically urged Pittsburgh-area viewers to support Pat financially.

During this time, I was reminded of one of my favorite verses: "...'But what shall we do about the hundred talents which I have given to the army of Israel?' The man of God answered, 'The Lord is able to give you much more than this' " (2 Chronicles 25:9).

Since then, we have always given freely to other Christian television ministries, expecting nothing in return except the blessing of God.

A s I've stated, Pat and I had an oral agreement that he would run *The 700 Club* on our station. However, as things progressed, it seemed that he changed his mind. I was deeply hurt and very angry at this response. I called Pat and begged him to pray about it.

Finally, with my eyes filled with tears, I sat down at my type-writer. I wrote Pat a six-page letter defending myself for what I had done right, apologizing for what I had done wrong, and insisting that Pat keep our oral agreement.

I folded the letter, sealed and stamped it, and walked to the corner mailbox. As I left the house, I heard a Voice in my spirit: "*I* am your Vindication!"

I ignored the Voice. Again came that word: "*I* am your Vindication!"

"Well, You're doing a terrible job of vindicating me!" I remarked and continued walking toward the mailbox.

"*I* am your Vindication!"

"No! I've got to defend the truth!"

"*I* am your Vindication!"

"Then *why* haven't You been vindicating me?"

"*I* am your Vindication!"

By this time I was at the mailbox.

I pulled open the door. A sixth time—once for each page perhaps: "*I* am your Vindication!"

I stood there, holding the mailbox door, arguing with myself and with the Lord. "God, if You were my Vindication, You would have gotten Pat Robertson's attention!"

In my heart I knew whose Voice it was, and my fear of God overruled my anger and indignation.

I released the mailbox and turned away, the letter still in my sweating hand.

"Well, You'd *better* be my Vindication!" I said and walked stiffly back home.

For weeks afterward I battled with overwhelming rage.

"I know I've got to forgive Pat, or the Lord won't do anything for me," I told myself.

The Bible commands Christians to forgive anyone whom we feel has abused or mistreated us. If we don't forgive, God can't bless us. (Besides, there is always an element of misunderstanding in every dispute.)

All these conflicting thoughts raced through my mind as I struggled to forgive Pat. The enormity of what I perceived as his offense against us would often well up in my consciousness, flooding me with anger and resentment.

This experience taught me something about forgiveness. I realized that sometimes we have to forgive the other person every day—even many times a day—as often as "seventy times seven." I also learned that forgiveness is not something you feel; it is something you do.

Jesus never commanded us to forgive and forget, just forgive.

I couldn't forget. At times, I was aware of it all day as Satan continued to beat me over the head with the matter. Occasionally, the rage would begin to overwhelm me before I could recognize who was behind it.

Every time I had to *will* myself to forgive Pat.

*S*urely *things can't get any worse*, I told myself. But I was wrong.

During the time I was struggling to forgive Pat, I clung to the faint hope that he would keep his commitment to us—simply because I trusted his integrity.

Pat had earlier told me that I should be able to finance the major equipment purchases for Channel 22 through RCA Corporation. He had said, "I have made purchases from them with only ten percent down—and even once with no money down."

With that fact in mind, I made a proposal to RCA. After all, we had to buy our major broadcast equipment within 18 months or lose the Construction Permit for Channel 22.

I phoned the sales manager at RCA and explained about our 120 Club and the fact that people were contributing monthly to our 3,000 Club.

"I want 75 percent down!" the sales manager abruptly informed me.

"Seventy-five percent?" I argued. "But you've made deals with CBN for ten percent down!"

The man was as cold and hard as steel; he wouldn't budge.

My emotional roller coaster took another precipitous dip.

Later we found out that as a result of some heated discussion, a CBN executive decided to contact the sales manager at RCA about us. Later this executive sought me out and apologized for his actions. But the damage had been done.

Not long after the RCA incident, one of my best friends in Pittsburgh, Charles Bowlin, went to Virginia Beach on vacation to visit *The 700 Club*. (I tell this story with Charles' kind permission.)

After the program, Charles had the opportunity to talk with Pat Robertson and asked, "Are you going to put *The 700 Club* on Russ Bixler's station when he gets it built?"

Pat's negative reply was all Charles needed to hear.

After returning home from Virginia, Charles called our new pastor and said, "I'd like to set up a meeting with you, the chairman of your deacons, and Russ."

(At the Lord's instruction, I had resigned as pastor of the Pittsburgh Church of the Brethren three years earlier in 1972.)

I was totally in the dark about the reason for the meeting.

Charles told the three of us what had transpired in Virginia Beach and then said sharply, "You lied to us, Russ."

After recovering from my initial shock, I responded to Charles, "Now here's what really happened," and I detailed the events of the past several years.

"Pat says you don't have a contract with CBN."

"Contract? Of course we don't have a contract! We're both Christians, and we had an oral agreement!" I explained. "In fact, the whole television project was his idea!"

Charles still insisted that I was lying.

I could understand why he felt that way. Charles was simply reacting to Pat Robertson's response.

Our deacon chairman, who had known me for 15 years, didn't accept Charles' statement. "I believe Russ," he said.

The pastor was torn and didn't know what to believe, although he continued to support me.

Charles Bowlin left the meeting and began a systematic effort to discredit me. He called many of the pastors who he thought were my friends.

Later I learned that some of them were quite interested in what Charles had to say. One, my dear Presbyterian friend, John Blewitt, however, retorted promptly, "I don't believe that about Russ Bixler!"

Helen Mierski, who attended the same Episcopal congregation as the Bowlins, told Charles, "I don't believe what you're saying about Russ!" She became known irreverently as a "Bixler girl." Other people were teased and ridiculed for the same reason.

Charles went to our accountant and demanded that the books be audited. "Russ Bixler is stealing money from the ministry!" he charged.

The accountant immediately responded, "Russ can't be stealing money since I have control of the checkbook."

Charles didn't believe that, either.

It is true that many people would place money in my hand or shove it in my coat pocket, but I have always been diligent to give to the television ministry every penny I have ever received for that purpose. That's what made Charles' accusation doubly painful. And to think he'd been one of my best friends!

I could hardly blame Charles; Pat Robertson's reply to him had the ring of certainty and finality to it. Charles was simply trying to be a Christian statesman, protecting the Christian community from a rip-off.

A woman in Pittsburgh heard this rumor and decided to write to Pat Robertson. He responded with a letter that confirmed what Charles Bowlin had been saying in that *The 700*

Club would not be carried on our station. I was told that she made copies of the letter and distributed them widely within the Christian community.

When friends would ask me, "Are these accusations true?" I would tell them what had really occurred.

If my defense got carried back to Charles Bowlin, he would launch another verbal attack against me.

One day Charles, who is a contractor, slipped while working on a roof and fell to the ground. Although he could have been killed, he actually only suffered some painful bruises.

About the same time a drunk driver slammed head-on into Charles' new pickup truck. The police found Charles a quarter of a mile down the highway, suffering from a concussion and totally unaware of what was happening.

Charles' business began to deteriorate. As a good manager and a hard worker, he had always been on top of things. Eventually Charles suffered a nervous breakdown and was able only to work part-time for a period. He also had to have painful surgery for polyps in his sinuses.

Although I had long since forgiven Charles, I began to feel sorry for him. Not only were Norma and I praying for Pat Robertson and supporting CBN financially, but we were now praying rather earnestly for Charles Bowlin.

"Why doesn't Charles call me to try to get this mess cleared up?" I wondered.

One afternoon I felt a nudge from the Holy Spirit, so I phoned the Bowlins. When Lavona Bowlin heard my voice, she almost cried, "Oh, Russell! Please do come this evening!"

Lavona also invited another Christian couple. When I arrived, the two women went to the basement, leaving me with Charles and his friend.

Immediately Charles began to cry and fell on his knees in front of me. "Please take this curse off me! Please forgive me! Get this off my back; I can't stand it any more!"

"Charles, I've long since forgiven you. Now *receive* your forgiveness."

The two of us placed our hands on Charles and prayed for him.

As far as I could discern, Charles appeared to be totally healed—instantly. His business began picking up, and we became good friends once again. In fact, to this day we meet together for dinner, and Charles occasionally uses me as a pastor-counselor. We genuinely love each other.

Forgiveness is the key.

During this same period, CBN was also experiencing serious setbacks. One of Pat's executives later told me how difficult their financial situation became at that time.

By airing *The 700 Club* on Channel 53, Pat got some of the money we would have received from supporters in the Pittsburgh area, but he probably suffered even greater losses overall.

Forgiveness is an act that must have legs. In other words, "Love is something you do!"

I invited Pat Robertson to be the keynote speaker for the 1975 Greater Pittsburgh Charismatic Conference. Pat was quite reserved when we met.

Into the Teeth of the Blizzard

During the opening session at Pittsburgh's great Civic Arena, I introduced Pat with as eloquent and complimentary a statement as I could prepare. This introduction seemed to warm his heart, and Pat and I hugged each other in front of nearly 10,000 cheering Christians.

Several years later, Pat came to Pittsburgh as our studio was under construction. He looked over what we were doing, and then he apologized to Norma and me.

To this day Pat Robertson and I remain good friends. From the moment WPCB-TV went on the air, he befriended us. Our ministry would not have survived without Pat's liberal assistance.

I didn't see how we could possibly purchase the expensive television equipment for Channel 22 with just a few months left in our agreement with Julian Smith. We could have afforded a 10 percent down payment—but 75 percent down? We were not even close.

As a result of the rumors concerning our disagreement about *The 700 Club,* one-third of the members of our 120 Club withdrew their money—causing us to lose many thousands of dollars.

Why can't we raise more money? The thought went through my mind every day.

The Lord had promised Norma that He would provide, and we were praying. But the money was just "dribbling in."

During this time, a group of other "potential Christian broadcasters"—men who were also trying to build Christian television stations in various eastern cities—decided to get together to share helpful information among ourselves. At the meeting we made reports to each other.

One man who seemed to have it all together gave a glowing report about his construction, then concluded with, "But I can't tell you anything about raising money; you'll have to find out about fund-raising from Russ Bixler!"

I nearly fell off my chair! I had come to the meeting hoping that the other men would tell *me* how to get the money we needed.

If they think I know what I'm doing, I said to myself, *we must all be in over our heads!*

E very time something terrible would happen, Norma developed a "knot" in her stomach. She couldn't eat and felt miserable.

One day she went into the bedroom and got on her knees. "Lord, I know that You told us to build this station, but I just can't take the pressure," Norma prayed. "I refuse to accept this knot in my stomach any more." When she got off her knees, the knot was gone, and it never returned.

In early 1976, Norma suggested that I keep a diary of the miracles God was doing in our lives. And there were lots of healing miracles.

"That's a great idea," I agreed.

Every night, as I wrote the day's events in the diary, I would try to include something that deserved a "Praise the Lord!"

Into the Teeth of the Blizzard

As the months of 1976 passed, the praiseworthy events became fewer and fewer; only disasters were available to record in my diary.

"Lord, You gave us Isaiah 49:22: 'I will raise my signal to the peoples.' Was that some kind of sick joke?"

Frankly, I was irritated at God for not warning me about how serious the warfare was going to be. It had become a much more forceful "blizzard" than I had ever walked into before.

I simply had not taken seriously Pat Robertson's word of warning: "Building a Christian television station is like walking into the teeth of a blizzard. The wind and snow make walking quite difficult, but it cannot stop you. Only *you* can stop you! You must keep walking."

God had indeed warned, but I had not been listening.

Finally, by the month of May, I simply could not maintain the diary any longer, and I gave up in total discouragement. My heart was broken.

I didn't know the initial breakthrough would occur before the end of that very month.

Chapter 3

What I Really Wanted to Do

My reputation was nearly destroyed in Pittsburgh. Yet in our personal ministry, Norma and I were seeing miracles in quantity and power greater than ever before.

In large numbers Roman Catholics were coming to our church, where until 1976 I was still leading the Sunday evening service on a voluntary basis. On Sundays we hosted a number of international visitors, including a sizable delegation of French Lutheran and Reformed pastors.

I was also receiving invitations to minister across North America and in Europe. Sten Nilsson of Uppsala, Sweden, asked us to minister in several Swedish churches.

A German surgeon who had visited our church told Pastor Siegfried Müller of Karlsruhe, Germany, that he should invite us to minister to his congregation. "Make sure you invite Norma, too," the doctor insisted.

Pastor Müller, a very energetic and ambitious man, decided to fly to Pittsburgh to check us out.

During that Sunday evening service Norma gave a very specific word: "God is healing somebody's right hand in the church in Germany!"

Everyone stared at Siegfried, and he flushed a bit.

The next day we invited Siegfried to our home for dinner, and he came with questions about Norma's word of knowledge.

Norma added, "I only know that it's someone who loves you very much."

The next Sunday morning, Pastor Müller stepped into his pulpit in Karlsruhe, Germany, and repeated the word of knowledge about a right hand being healed. A long, embarrassing pause ensued while the congregation wondered what had happened to their pastor while he was in America.

"Does someone here have a problem with a right hand?" Siegfried, a typical German, stubbornly persisted.

Finally, a very short man stood up. This farmer and his wife live many miles from Karlsruhe, but they love Pastor Müller so much that, whenever they can, they leave home before dawn to drive to his church.

The farmer held up his right hand and said, "I have a very painful right hand. In fact, I'm going to the hospital Thursday for surgery. But it's not hea.... It's *healed*!" he screamed, shaking his right hand in front of the congregation!

Word of that miracle spread to other German-speaking churches where we were scheduled to minister, so they were eagerly waiting

The German farmer whose hand was healed.

for Norma and me to arrive. As a result of their faith, we saw miracles of a magnitude such as we had never seen before.

O n that ministry tour, we included a number of churches in Sweden. Miracles were taking place everywhere we went—until we arrived at a Baptist church in Karlstad. Those Swedish Baptists folded their arms and questioned everything that sounded miraculous.

The pastor, who was Spirit-filled, was quite frustrated by the lack of response. Norma and I knew that people were being healed by God's power, but they would not acknowledge their miracles.

During the next-to-last evening in Karlstad, the Lord told me that He had great plans for this Swedish pastor (these plans have long since been fulfilled), and He instructed me to go up to the pulpit and pray for him.

I got up from the front pew, reached over to my interpreter (a college student majoring in English), and took her by the hand. She walked behind the pastor to the "interpreter's microphone" while I placed my hand on his forehead. I began to pray into his microphone and quickly went into a prophecy describing how this pastor would have a nationwide ministry. He was crying rather profusely when I returned to my seat.

After the service, two men—a father and his son—asked if I could speak Swedish. I laughed and said, "Of course not."

The father responded, "When you had your hand on the pastor's head, you were speaking in perfect Swedish!"

"Aw, you just heard the interpreter," I suggested.

"Do you think I can't tell the difference between a man's voice and a woman's voice? It was *you,* wasn't it?"

The son nodded in agreement.

The father motioned to his son, who then gathered some other men. Every one of them affirmed that I had spoken in Swedish.

I looked for Norma and saw a group of women standing around her. "Norma, these men all say that I was prophesying in Swedish. What did you hear?"

"I only heard English, but these women are also saying that you were speaking in Swedish."

When we asked the pastor, he said, "I heard English." His wife, however, said, "The prophecy was mostly, but not all, Swedish." The interpreter said it was all English.

Sten Nilsson, who had been seated on the front pew beside Norma, asserted with awe in his voice, "Every foreigner who comes to Sweden, no matter how many years he has lived here, always betrays his foreignness by his accent. You spoke Swedish as if you had been *born* here!"

Yet I had prophesied in English! Everybody went home all abuzz over the remarkable miracle they had heard.

Norma and I ministered one more evening in the church in Karlstad, and that night all heaven caved in on those stuffy Baptists! They had all witnessed an astonishing miracle, so their hearts were prepared.

Some years later, the Swedish pastor and his wife shared on Cornerstone TeleVision the aftereffects of that miracle service. "We received calls, letters, and visits—averaging one per day, for at least two weeks—affirming previously unreported miracles among the congregation, plus some additional miracles among the visitors from the community."

What I Really Wanted to Do

For nearly a year, I thought I was the only Christian who had ever experienced such a "language" miracle. Then I began to discover that this miracle takes place occasionally on the foreign mission field. God does it to gain the attention of unbelievers.

Called *akolalia,* this phenomenon occurs when a foreigner speaks in his own language, but the Holy Spirit causes the natives to hear the message in their language. Speaking from personal experience, I know it makes an incredible impact!

Although we witnessed great miracles in Sweden and Germany, these were minimal compared to what we saw in Switzerland, the land of my forefathers.

When I preached in the capital, Bern, I reminded the Swiss that my ancestor, Ulrich Bichsel, had been burned at the stake right there in Bern. "I hope you treat me better than you treated my ancestor!" I joked.

A second of uncomfortable silence was suddenly followed by uproarious laughter!

The Swiss promptly accepted me as one of their own, which is quite unusual for a proud people living in the most beautiful country in the world. The miracles were so numerous in Switzerland that we could hardly keep track of them.

I had also received an invitation to preach in a church in Strasbourg, France—the 100-year-old Le Temple Neuf, which, next to the huge Cathedral, is the largest church in Strasbourg.

The French government, however, had other ideas. Although Charles de Gaulle had already died, his spirit lived on through countless Francophiles who refused permission for me to preach there.

One of the French pastors who had visited our church in Pittsburgh and seen us in action drove to Paris and successfully interceded with French officials for us. I was unaware of this hostile situation until we arrived.

The pastor of Le Temple Neuf had a son, also a Lutheran pastor, serving a church in another part of France. Suffering from a terrible stomach ulcer, the son arrived in Strasbourg at the same time Norma and I did. The young pastor was going to stay overnight with his parents and enter the hospital in Strasbourg for tests the next morning. Stomach surgery was in his future.

As the three of them were eating dinner, the older pastor told his son, "An American with a healing ministry is speaking at our church this evening. Would you like to attend?"

"What!" the son exploded. "You invited a healer to Le Temple Neuf? Are you crazy in your old age?"

"Well, I know what you think, but Pastor Bixler comes highly recommended."

"I can't believe my own father would fall for such a scam!"

"Well, won't you just attend this evening, and then let me know what you think?"

The young pastor reluctantly agreed.

That evening the pastor introduced me and walked back to his seat near the altar, another 40 feet or so behind me. The pulpit was so far from the congregation that I could hardly see the people behind the first few rows in that huge, dark building. I was all alone, with my amplified voice reverberating off the great stone walls.

At the end of my message I asked Norma what God was doing, and she shouted loud enough for me to hear, "He's healing a stomach ulcer."

"Who's being healed of a stomach ulcer?" I asked into the microphone.

No one stirred. "You're probably feeling very warm right now," I said some moments later.

At last a hand went up in the third row.

"C'est mon fils!" screamed the pastor behind me. "C'est mon fils!" ("That's my son!")

We later learned that the heat of the Holy Spirit had been coursing up and down the young pastor's body until it stopped in his stomach.

On the third evening of ministry, the pastor made an announcement to the congregation. "My son called to report that the doctors could find nothing; he is totally healed!"

Strasbourg was another memorable experience!

I almost dreaded coming home.

I told Norma, "Our ministry is established nationally and internationally. Maybe we should move away from Pittsburgh."

Norma was alarmed. She prayed, "Lord, what can I do to help? After all, I'm the one You gave the initial vision."

The Lord spoke promptly, "You are to get together a group of women who know how to pray."

"But all the women who know how to pray are busy."

"Have you asked them yet?"

"Well, no."

Norma got on the phone and invited six other women who knew how to pray in power. Every one of them agreed to participate in a weekly prayer meeting for the television station. It was open warfare.

Those women, later affectionately known as the Super Seven, literally prayed WPCB-TV on the air. In fact, they still meet for prayer—nearly 25 years later.

There is absolutely no way I could have built this ministry without Norma. She has stood solidly behind me all along this difficult road, even when she disagreed with something I was doing.

Norma has stated many times that she was afraid of arriving in heaven and hearing Jesus ask her, "Why did you quit?"

Chapter 4

Harassments and Hallelujahs

Loren Cunningham, founder of Youth With a Mission and Mercy Ships—among the world's largest missions organizations—had been invited to teach daily at the May 1976 Greater Pittsburgh Charismatic Conference. He also was scheduled to give the main address for the final session on Saturday evening.

"Is someone building a Christian television station in Pittsburgh?" Loren asked Norma.

"Why, yes," Norma confirmed. "In fact, my own husband is spearheading the project."

"You're kidding!" Loren exclaimed. "On the plane coming to Pittsburgh, I was praying about my Saturday evening message when the Spirit of God told me about a Christian TV station in Pittsburgh—even the number of the television channel."

"That's wonderful!" Norma replied, trying to control her enthusiasm.

"In fact," Loren continued, "the Holy Spirit has directed me to take an offering for the television ministry at that final service."

The Planning Committee for the conference agreed, and Norma and I began to feel our first bit of God's vindication—just two weeks after I had quit writing in my diary out of sheer discouragement.

I had never heard Loren Cunningham teach, so I took an hour or so from my administrative duties to visit his teaching session. The Holy Spirit surely led in my choice of class to attend.

Loren described—with appropriate biblical illustrations—how the Lord may speak to a person to fulfill a certain project, and then disaster hits. Loren went on to describe scripturally how the Lord will later raise the devastated project out of the ashes and hasten its completion. Then he told how this had happened concerning his vision of Mercy Ships.

He's talking about ***me!*** I thought.

A joy exploded in my heart! The television station was back on course, and I knew it!

Loren Cunningham preached on Saturday evening about Gideon. When this mighty warrior spread a garment to receive the spoils of battle, the victorious Israelites threw the gold, silver, and jewelry they had taken in the fight. The value of the spoils, according to Judges 8, totaled 1,700 shekels of gold.

Loren preached on this offering concept from Gideon, then placed three blankets at the front of the auditorium, and invited everyone to come forward and give a gift to help build WPCB-TV.

Loren Cunningham, founder of Youth With a Mission and Mercy Ships, 1976.

46

Harassments and Hallelujahs

"In addition to cash and checks," Loren suggested, "you may give pledges or jewelry and other items that can be turned into cash."

Folks were walking up, hugging and patting me on the back, and congratulating me. A pastor who had spoken against me (and I against him), came to me and held my hand for a time, and God resolved a long-standing breach between us.

While the offering was being counted, a man walked up and said, "I know how much is in that offering!"

"How do you know that?"

"The Living Bible gives the value of Gideon's offering in American dollars. It says 25,000 dollars."

When everything had been totaled, there was more than $22,000, plus some jewelry and pledges—probably very close to that figure from Judges 8:26.

I knew now that nothing could stop us.

At the same time, however, I still failed to realize how much Satan hates Christian television and the extreme lengths to which the devil will go to try to block the construction of a Christian TV station.

Jim Bakker had just completed his PTL facilities in Charlotte, and he invited supporters to a July 4th dedication. Pat Robertson was scheduled to speak, and so was I.

Pat received a warm welcome from the PTL viewers in the studio, and everybody saw some healing take place in the strained relationship between Pat and Jim Bakker. Paul and Jan Crouch of the Trinity Broadcasting Network were also there; additional healing occurred in that formerly severed relationship.

The dedication of PTL, 1976. From left to right: Jim Bakker, Russ, James Thompson of WGGS-TV, Greenville, South Carolina, Owen Carr of WCFC-TV, Chicago, and Bill Holt of the PTL Club's Board of Directors (background).

Why do Christian leaders often fail to get along with each other? I believe it stems from the fact that they are all pioneers, or visionaries. Such persons seldom agree among themselves. Each one *has* to be the leader, so they sometimes turn on each other.

This is a primary reason why the Texans lost the Battle of the Alamo. They had three very strong-willed pioneers among the defenders—Davy Crockett, Jim Bowie, and Colonel William B. Travis. Three headstrong men all trying to lead one group of defenders resulted in chaos.

Even the apostle Paul—a true visionary—always had to work where no one else was evangelizing.

Yet, without visionaries—pioneers, if you will—very little gets done in war as well as in the Kingdom of God. Jesus knew that such conflict was not limited to worldly trailblazers and gave His disciples this warning: "But it shall not be so among you; but whoever would be great among you must be your servant,

and whoever would be first among you must be slave of all"
(Mark 10:43-44).

Meanwhile, Norma's Super Seven became quite effective commandos in God's army and literally began tearing up Satan's kingdom. The women perceived their God-given duty as all-out warfare.

The Super Seven prayer group. From left to right: Norma, Nona Knerler, Barbara Conner, Maxine George, Lenore Boering, Pauline Walton,

I had felt so alone for so long that they provided for me a very comforting feeling of security and strength.

One day, a wonderful Christian friend, Glen McElwain, was in the bank when the teller, Eleanor Blazevich, asked him, "Does Russ Bixler need a hilltop for the Christian television station?"

"Why do you ask?" Glen wondered. As the area representative for *The 700 Club,* he was interested in anything regarding the new station.

"I know of a hill near my home in Wall Borough that is available."

Glen gave me the information, and I followed it up.

Until her recent retirement, Eleanor worked for Cornerstone TeleVision—on that very hilltop—only a few hundred yards from her home. She and her husband, Lt. Joseph Blazevich of the county sheriff's department, seemed to have the same vision as Norma and I.

"**L**et's have a telethon on Channel 53," I suggested to the Board of Directors.

As Pittsburgh's only independent station, Channel 53 was already carrying *The 700 Club,* as well as other CBN-produced programs.

"We must get the word out to the community so Christians in the area can assist in providing financial support."

Our Board agreed, so I visited the owner of Channel 53, a very gracious Jewish businessman named Henry Posner.

"That's fine with me," he said, "but we have a problem. Our contract with CBN stipulates that Pat Robertson has the right to veto any program we schedule during the hour before CBN's programs and the half-hour following."

Mr. Posner and Bill Smith, his vice president, a precious Christian gentleman, flew to Norfolk to ask Pat Robertson if he would allow us to put our telethon in those time slots during the weekend after Labor Day of 1976.

Pat did not permit it; he thought that the viewers might confuse our efforts with *The 700 Club.* And he had a point. The two men returned to Pittsburgh deeply disappointed. So we scheduled the telethon at all the hours we could—two here, three there—through the Labor Day weekend.

Meanwhile, we had negotiated an oral deal to lease the land Eleanor Blazevich had suggested for our transmitting site. The owner, however, decided that he would rather sell it. He was asking more than $50,000.

We agreed to purchase the land, not having any idea where we would get $50,000-plus.

When our Board of Directors decided to have a telethon to raise money for WPCB-TV, we looked at each other: "Do you know how to do a telethon?"

"No, don't you?"

I called the *PTL Club,* and asked if I could visit to learn how to produce a telethon. They were very gracious, so one of our volunteers flew with me to Charlotte.

"Have you ever seen the *PTL Club* program?" I asked my companion.

"No, but I'd like to watch it," he replied.

We went into the area reserved for the spectators, taking the *last two* available seats, right on the front row. As Jim Bakker and co-host Henry Harrison came into the studio to do the program, Jim spotted me. He asked Henry if I was on the program, but Henry didn't know. Jim asked the producer, and she told him I wasn't, so he just waved at me.

As the *PTL Club* opened, Jim Bakker abruptly told everybody that the Holy Spirit had just spoken to him. "God is telling me to take an offering for the station in Pittsburgh! Everybody! Send one dollar to Pittsburgh! What's your address, Russ?"

The producer quickly ran over and got our address. Jim started walking around the studio, holding up everybody for one dollar. And I mean *everybody*! He demanded that each one in the studio audience give me a dollar, so they started stuffing dollar bills in my pocket. And they didn't even know who I was! A few people gave 10- or 20-dollar bills.

Later, when Norma watched the videotape of that program, she commented, "You were as pale as a ghost."

Jim kept repeating the request for dollar bills: "I've *never* had God speak to me more forcefully! This station is of God! Everybody! Send one dollar to the address on the screen! This station will be a lighthouse for the Lord!"

I knew God had reserved those last two seats on the front row!

Back in Pittsburgh our little post office box was quickly jammed, and the postmaster delivered the mail to us in large bags. Several of our Board members suggested that their children help open the mail, and they loved it. The dollar bills poured in for weeks!

When the flow finally stopped, we had heard from all 50 states and received a total of more than $50,000—in one dollar bills! God had given us the money for the land to build the station!

We scheduled a prayer and praise meeting and invited our supporters to the hill. We cut a temporary road through the jungle-like underbrush—and we didn't even own the property yet!

Only a four-wheel drive vehicle could make it to the top. We gave everybody a choice: Wait for your turn to ride in the truck or walk the steep hill. A surprising number walked up through the brush.

How thrilled I was to see so many Christians standing with me!

Harassments and Hallelujahs

I sent out a newsletter to our mailing list, inviting volunteers to help with the telethon on Channel 53.

One day I returned home from hours of preparation, when Norma said, "I've been taking calls all day long. Here are the volunteers who phoned today."

She handed me a sheet of legal paper with one-and-a-half columns of names, each one with a phone number.

"This name with the check mark by it...," Norma pointed out. "I don't know who she is, but the Lord says she's very important!" The name of that volunteer—chosen by God out of more than 50—was Oleen Eagle!

I opened a letter one day to see a check for $15,000. A friend who was being promoted to vice president of his company had to move from Pittsburgh. He and his wife agreed that if the Lord would sell their house for $150,000, they would give one-tenth to the television ministry. The first person to look at the house promptly wrote out a check without quibbling. So we received the tenth, $15,000.

Any discerning Christian could see by now that the television project was a miracle ministry. Yet disasters were happening at the same time.

Julian Smith took us to Federal court because we didn't have all our equipment purchased within the required 18 months, and we lost the case. However, the settlement stipulated that he reimburse us for whatever equipment purchases we had made and other out-of-pocket expenses.

We lost the court case, but the settlement gave us more than $200,000 in desperately needed funds to replace out-of-pocket expenditures.

This meant that we had to give up the Construction Permit for Channel 22 and re-apply for Channel 40 at the Federal

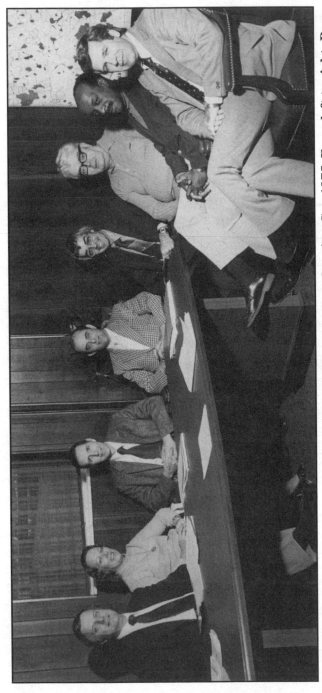

The Board of Directors of Western Pennsylvania Christian Broadcasting Co., 1975. From left to right: Russ, Luena Darr (secretary), Ernie Frederick, Dick West, George Kemp, Charles Schieb (attorney), Michael Adams, James Steele.

Communications Commission. All that wasted publicity—first for Channel 53, then for Channel 22—down the drain!

The emotional roller coaster was extremely stressful for me. And every change meant another painful and expensive delay. I was fed up with the delays!

Still, I felt a bit of confidence. I now had three multi-millionaires—all Christians—who had pledged to support the station. One, however, welshed on his pledge and didn't give a penny! An unscrupulous preacher got to the second with a con-cocted story about me, so that millionaire bailed out, too. The third one made a couple of nominal contributions and then walked away.

I was devastated! "God! What's going on?"

The Lord answered: "You thought you were secure because you had three multi-millionaires in your hip pocket. *Now* you have to depend upon Me!"

What a hard lesson! That's when I began to appreciate "the little people"—those innumerable but very faithful Christians who give what little they can every month.

W e put together an army of volunteers for that tele-thon on Channel 53—those who would answer tele-phones, and those who would type, keep records, or do any one of a myriad of tasks involved in a telethon. And they were *all* volunteers!

I had heard about Stan Scott, the former atheist newscaster from Channel 9 who had gotten saved, so I phoned him.

Stan prayed about it, and the Lord spoke: "Help Russ Bixler!" And he did; Stan gave freely of his time during the planning and execution of the telethon. He gave it a strong touch of professionalism.

Roger McDuff came in from Texas to sing for us.

The telethon was hard work, but it was fun, too.

The staff at Channel 53 demanded that we format *every second* of that weekend, and they didn't want us to vary from it.

Oleen Eagle, who was given the job of volunteer producer, began to write with the strangest sensation. It was as if she were being guided through the entire format. Yet she had never done anything like that before! Oleen had the clear sense that God was working a miracle through her.

Nancy Thomas, Helen Mierski, and Joanne Kline were volunteer typists, and Oleen kept all three of them busy for hours.

Henry Posner, the owner of Channel 53, also owned an outdoor advertising company. He agreed to put up billboards advertising the telethon all around the Greater Pittsburgh area, giving us a nice discount on the signs. But there was one thing we hadn't considered: If you want a good billboard, you've got to pick out the location yourself. Since 1976 was a presidential election year, the most visible billboards had already been taken.

When Norma and I went driving around to look for some of our signs, she would exclaim, "Look, Russell! There's one!"

"Where? I can't see it."

Literally, we had wasted the Lord's money. Very few people acknowledged that they had seen the billboards. Most of them were isolated, or so high that they could hardly be read.

I told the Board of Directors that we had to order the expensive television equipment *before* the telethon, or the Lord wouldn't bless our fund-raising. It was a truth I just *knew*!

The other Board members disagreed; they wanted to see the pledges to pay for the equipment before they would order it.

"But don't you see the financial miracles the Lord has been doing for us?" I argued. "Look at the miracle of the *PTL Club* offering! This job will be delayed two years if we don't step out on faith!"

They still wouldn't budge. This time it was not an outside problem but, rather, the enemy had infiltrated our house—the Board of Directors.

The rest of the Board met without me during the telethon and agreed that we were not receiving enough pledges to risk ordering the equipment. When the telethon was ended I confronted them with their unbelief, and we had a king-sized "blowup."

They all resigned except dear Ernie Frederick.

Later Ernie got down on his knees in front of Norma and me, asking us to forgive him. Ernie made a 180-degree turn, and for about 15 years thereafter was the most valuable Board member we ever enjoyed.

But it was too late. I knew in my heart that if we didn't order the equipment before the telethon, we wouldn't receive enough money. And it did delay us an additional two years.

The telethon itself was exciting; people got saved and healed; some were filled with the Holy Spirit. Many pledges were phoned in, but not as much as we expected. However, part of the Christian community learned that we were building a Christian television station.

After the telethon more Christians joined the spiritual warfare in prayer, yet most pastors remained on the sidelines. To this day I cannot understand that attitude.

Many pastors say that Christian television is "shallow," and to a degree they are correct. But they don't realize that average Americans know almost nothing about the Bible; their knowledge of God is woefully deficient. Presenting theology over their heads would be counter-productive, and highly informative programing is usually too expensive for Christian stations.

Pat Robertson at Cornerstone TeleVision, 1989.

Even in the Church, few American Christians have truly learned what it means to "walk in the Spirit." Christian television has to reach people where they are—and they are not seminary-trained, as are most pastors.

The struggle to gain support remained frustrating; in a very real sense, we were stalled again.

Then I met a friend downtown. "My leasing company will purchase the transmitter and lease it to you," he told me.

Harassments and Hallelujahs

An out-of-town bank offered us a similar deal for the cameras and miscellaneous broadcast equipment.

I was learning that something good always followed each disaster. Once again the project began to roll, and we began site preparation.

Watching the big tower sections roll in on long trucks excited all of us. The electric company, however, was not willing to erect and string poles for a mile and a half when they weren't sure the station would even get on the air.

"We have to have electricity!" I told Norma. "This is a project for your prayer group." In prayer these warriors "commanded" the electric company to provide electricity.

One day the seven women decided to come up on our hill to continue their spiritual warfare. When they arrived, they followed another vehicle up the hill. They realized that it was the truck carrying the electric poles!

The Lord had indeed caused the local electric company to change their minds, but an even greater problem simmered just below the surface.

Beneath our hill lies a coal mine. In fact, the mine floor is no more than 50 feet underground. Today a mining company would strip away the hill, but not a century ago. Mine subsidence occurs throughout Western Pennsylvania because of extensive shallow mining activity in the past.

This meant we had to sink a number of large concrete and steel caissons to the mine floor. The tower required three 48-inch-diameter caissons, and the transmitter building needed eight caissons of the same size.

In addition, the three concrete anchors that held the long guy wires for the tower were huge. You can imagine the cost of such an enormous project. At one point we had more money invested underground than above ground!

Drilling the huge holes for the foundation, 1977.

Out of nowhere, I received a petition that had been filed at the Federal Communications Commission, opposing the swap of Channel 40 for 22.

"Oh, no! Months more of delay!"

The petition was not aimed at us, but at Julian Smith. Since we were a party to the channel swap, the entire deal ground to a total halt.

"God! I can't take any more of this!" I could hardly sleep that night.

Family after family dropped their support; they found it hard to believe that a project ordained by God could experience so many roadblocks.

At the same time, however, additional Christians would replace those who had fallen away. Our monthly support remained stable at about $23,000.

One day I received a check for about $12,000 from a lawyer who was obviously angry. A Christian lady we didn't know had changed her will to include the Western Pennsylvania Christian Broadcasting Company, and then died shortly thereafter.

The attorney was so miffed that he wouldn't even give us the names of the heirs so we could express our appreciation. "They are angry, too!" was all he would tell us.

Once again, God's financial timing was exquisite.

"**W**e need some kind of television programing to keep the project in the public eye."

With that in mind, we decided to have a one-hour Saturday morning TV program called *Getting It Together* on Channel 53.

Getting It Together **at Channel 53. From left to right: Russ, Tibb Gethin, Peggy Hoffman, Stan Scott.**

Stan Scott felt that the Lord wanted him to continue to be involved; after all, Stan reminded us again, "God said, 'Help Russ Bixler.' "

I asked Oleen Eagle if she would like to be the producer of the program, so she became our first part-time employee.

During the summer prior to that telethon I had been invited to speak at JESUS '76, with many thousands of excited young Christians.

While I was there, a tall man with a marvelous speaking voice walked up to me and introduced himself. "Russ, I'm Bill Freeman of CBN. I've been wanting to meet you."

We chatted a while and then parted.

As I walked away, the Holy Spirit spoke, "Some day he will work with you!" I didn't forget it.

Getting It Together continued to plug along on Channel 53 each Saturday morning. From time to time on the air, Stan and I shared with our viewers the progress on our hilltop east of Pittsburgh. Oleen also arranged for guests to be interviewed.

For one hour every Saturday morning, volunteers answered the ten prayer phones located at the church I had pastored for 13 years, the Pittsburgh Church of the Brethren. Steve Totin organized the prayer partners.

One day a television director at Channel 53 came to me and said with some hostility, "Why are you playing this game? You know as well as I do that you can't afford to build a TV station!"

"Just watch us!" I retorted.

He walked off muttering something about "ripping off people for an impossible vision."

I felt that we should celebrate our new property with a groundbreaking service on the hilltop. We scheduled it for Sunday afternoon, April 17, 1977. Stan Scott agreed to be the speaker, and we borrowed a flatbed truck as a stage. (By this time we had cut a simple dirt road up the hill.)

I had a Saturday evening speaking engagement in Maryland, so our family spent the night with my parents in Westminster. On Sunday morning we casually packed up and left for Pittsburgh and the groundbreaking service.

Suddenly I realized that I had misjudged the time, so I drove a bit faster. Then it started to rain, which initially made the highway a bit slippery. Then I got a flat tire. My spare tire was a winter tread, which concerned me.

Norma and our boys were really praying. By that time, it was getting very late, so I drove faster. The next thing I saw was the flashing light of a Maryland State trooper, who gave me a ticket.

"Lord God, I can't take any more of this!"

As the rain became heavier, I drove as fast as I could without risking our safety. We listened to the weather forecast, which indicated that the Mid-Atlantic states were in the middle of an all-day rainstorm.

I prayed with Norma, my voice choking with grief, "Lord, I can't stand one more disappointment! In Jesus' name, I command that rain to stay away from our hilltop!"

About five minutes before we arrived, the rain suddenly stopped. As I drove up the dirt road, the sun broke out upon our little corner of Pennsylvania.

There was rain in every direction, but not a drop at the future site of WPCB-TV! The sun shone all the time we sang and prayed, and while Stan Scott spoke. His message was full of hope and encouragement.

Everybody took a shovel and dug up some dirt. We closed that glorious service and, as we got into our cars, the rain began falling again.

My tears had turned to tears of joy! God had given me my own personal miracle, and I would never again question His direction to build this Christian television station!

W e needed a trailer on the hill to use for office space. After asking hundreds of people (we also mentioned it on Channel 53), we finally heard from a young couple who lived so far north of Pittsburgh that they could not view Pittsburgh's Channel 53. Somehow having learned of our need, they gave us a house trailer that they couldn't sell. That trailer served us quite well until we junked it in 1995.

Finally, the FCC granted the Construction Permit for Channel 40, and we built as fast as we could.

Civil engineer George Kemp was the Construction Manager for the project, and he and his people, especially Bob Helmstadter, put a lot of love and energy into the work. George didn't receive nearly the amount of money for the job that he normally would have charged.

We also found a remarkable Christian named Harold McKamish. Like George Kemp, Harold would do anything he could for the Kingdom of God. His business was sheet metal, and he saved us many thousands of dollars on the construction of the first building. Harold organized some of the young men from Teen Challenge, and did they work! Both of these godly men, George and Harold, were members of our Board of Directors at different times.

Harassments and Hallelujahs

**Young men from Teen Challenge. Director
Dick Turgeon is third from right.**

We figured out how we could divide our 24-foot by 48-foot
transmitter building into two halves—one for the transmitter
and master control, and the other for the studio and prayer
partners.

I've often said that television doesn't tell the truth. That was
certainly true in our first little studio. The cameras actually
made that space appear much larger, even though we were
planning to have the talk set, the music set, two cameras, and
ten phone prayer partners in a room 24-foot by 24-foot. We felt
like the old woman who lived in a shoe.

Our "Come and See" Rally, 1978

Faith Works

I went to Charlotte again to meet with Jim Bakker.

"Would you loan us two of your engineers to construct the technical parts of the station?"

"Sure," Jim graciously agreed. He even paid their salaries.

The entire neighborhood watched with fascination as the tower climbed skyward. That's when I decided that all tower erectors are crazy; they climbed so high we could hardly see them. We spent a lot of time praying for those men.

I called Bill Freeman at CBN. "We'd like to have you come to Pittsburgh to be our General Manager," I said, holding my breath.

Bill wasn't interested.

The Holy Spirit, however, was working in Bill's heart, and he ultimately agreed to come.

After hiring new staff, paying for the tower and studio construction, and air time on Channel 53, we were quickly running out of money again.

Our bill at Channel 53 was over $75,000. As a result, *Getting It Together* had to be terminated, and Henry Posner graciously agreed to wait for the rest of his money.

Norma's prayer group was like a bunch of hounds on the scent. They excitedly accepted my list of prayer requests each week, went to battle, and *took* them for the Kingdom. Then they'd check off in their minds each project as it was completed.

They were an army eager for the spoils of battle!

Chapter 5

Destruction, Duplicity— and a Deep Freeze

A utumn 1978 saw the *PTL Club's* engineers, Wayne Fast and Allen McCarty—along with Steve Totin, who had been hired to help—busily assembling the television gear.

Wayne Fast and Allen McCarty, engineers on loan from the *PTL Club*.

The work had stalled, however, because the interior wiring was not completed. We tried desperately to find an electrician to do the wiring, but no one was available. Time was running out.

George Kemp found Jimmy Quinn, a young electrician who agreed to do the work alone.

"Everything is taking longer than it should," Wayne complained. "It's as if the job is just dragging along."

"It's a spiritual problem," Al concluded. "A satanic attack."

"Are you a Christian?" Steve asked Jimmy Quinn one day.

"No, I'm not," Jimmy admitted.

Right on the spot Steve led the young man to Jesus. From that point on, Jimmy became excited about the significance of his work. "This station will help others find Jesus and get saved, too!"

By October 18, 1978, we had made a decision.

"We are finally making progress," I told the staff. "But we have to get on air soon; we are running out of money. Let's set a target to be on air around Thanksgiving Day!"

The 800-foot tower was completed; the huge 50-foot Channel 40 antenna was on the top; and the transmission line was assembled all the way up the center of the tower to the base of the antenna. The transmitter and other sizable pieces of gear had been delivered.

Jimmy Quinn was working happily and enjoying his newfound relationship with the Lord. One day after Jimmy had finished drilling two four-inch holes to tie in the transmitter line, he was kneeling on the steel beam that held the

Jimmy Quinn hard at work.

Destruction, Duplicity—and a Deep Freeze

480-volt electrical cubicle box. Steve was assisting him from the floor. And then something happened that convinced all of us of Satan's power.

Jimmy's *three-inch-diameter* metal rule popped out of his shirt pocket and silently dropped through the *four-inch-diameter* hole in the electrical cubicle box. It didn't make a sound. Satan had picked Jimmy's pocket!

"Steve, I just dropped my rule."

"Where did it go?"

"I don't know. Oh, I see it," Jimmy responded. "It's sitting on the power buss."

"Can you get to it?"

"That's the problem, Steve. We don't have any cut-off for the electric power."

"I'll call the electric company!"

"Wait!" Jimmy answered quickly. "That's a major job, and they would charge us for it. I wonder if I can reach in and get it out."

"Be careful, Jim," warned Steve.

"I don't know how that rule got out of my pocket," Jimmy muttered as he knelt on the steel beam and reached around in front of the opening to the cubicle box. "But if it didn't cause any trouble going in, maybe I can get it out."

As he tried gently to lift the rule out, an enormous explosion occurred—right in Jimmy's face. Four hundred eighty volts of electricity shot up Jimmy's arm, through his body, out through his knee, and into the metal he was kneeling on.

Boom!

The explosion rocked the office trailer next door where Bill Freeman and I were working. Bill and I leaped out to see what had happened.

Inside the building huge flashes and explosions continued as the electrical short-circuit exploded again and again.

With a cloud of smoke behind him, Steve crawled on his hands and knees out of the darkened building. Only a miracle saved Jimmy's life. The explosions persisted, and the smoke billowed out the door.

Across the building from Jimmy and Steve and behind large crates of television gear, Wayne Fast had been talking on the phone at the time of the explosion. The lights immediately went out, leaving Wayne in the darkness and the smoke.

"Jesus, help me!" he called out in desperation.

While he was groping through the smoke-filled building, an arc of light suddenly appeared in front of Wayne. As he followed this light, it led him through the darkness, where he stumbled into a dazed Jimmy Quinn. Wayne pushed Jimmy toward the light, and they found the door.

"I believe we were guided by an angel," Wayne told us later.

Jimmy's face, hand, and forearm were badly burned.

I placed my hands on him and prayed. Then Steve and I put him in my car, and we raced to the hospital four miles away. To our surprise, Jimmy was rejoicing.

"Just think!" he shouted from the backseat. "If this had happened 12 days ago, I'd be burning in hell right now!" And then we knew Jimmy would be all right.

I left Steve and Jimmy at the hospital and hurried back to the station. The volunteer firemen were already on the scene. As I got out of the car, one last, loud explosion blew the door off the transformer outside the building. And then everything was quiet.

Destruction, Duplicity—and a Deep Freeze

"I called the electric company," Wayne informed me, "but there was no response."

Almost an hour had passed since the explosion.

Inside the building, the firemen were spraying their electrical fire extinguishers wherever they saw smoke.

Soon news trucks from all three network television stations arrived.

"What happened?" they asked, surveying the damage with their cameras.

As they interviewed me, I had conflicting feelings. I was thinking of God's goodness, and I was looking at Satan's worst.

Several hours later, at home, Norma and I switched from channel to channel, noting the different news accounts of the explosion and fire.

George Kemp examining the fire damage after the explosion. (Photo taken from KDKA-TV's broadcast.)

All the reporters were asking the same question: "Why did the power company not respond to the emergency calls from the station?" We learned later that the workers were changing shifts, and our call had fallen between the cracks.

"You know," I said to Norma, "some good may come out of this."

She agreed. "Now the whole community knows we're building a Christian television station!"

Still, I didn't sleep very well that night.

Faith Works

T he next morning we returned to a scene that reminded us of a terrible battlefield on the day after.

When we started to clean up, our attorney stopped us. "If you move anything," he warned, "the insurance company will blame the damage on you and refuse to reimburse the ministry."

Looking at that horrible mess day after day without being able to touch it became an extremely bitter experience. At the same time, God gave us some sweet moments of relief.

When I went to visit Jimmy Quinn in the hospital burn unit, he was remarkably joyful.

"Hey, Russ, I already saved one of the nurses!" he bubbled. As a new Christian, Jimmy didn't yet know how to describe the miracle of salvation.

During his recovery he became a favorite with the hospital staff, and his burns healed so rapidly that he was discharged several days earlier than expected. Prayer has a great effect on severe burns.

Finally the insurance company gave us permission to move the damaged equipment out of the building.

We tried to buy an old truck trailer for storage, but none could be found. The debris left from the 1978 Johnstown Flood had taken every old trailer within a 200-mile radius of Pittsburgh. At last a friend in eastern Pennsylvania found one and drove it to our hill.

The day the storage trailer arrived, a steady rain was falling, making paste out of the smoky dust.

"How are we ever going to clean up this mess?" we wondered aloud.

The dismal rain fit our mood.

Destruction, Duplicity—and a Deep Freeze

Just then a group of smiling Charismatic Catholics showed up in rain gear and promptly started carrying blackened equipment out to the trailer. They were like angels.

Not everyone we dealt with, however, had the same generous and helpful attitude.

When we totaled the damage, the insurance company made an offer of $100,000 *less*.

Disappointed and irritated by their hard-hearted coldness, I told their claim agent, "We ought to sue your company."

He just shrugged his shoulders.

"You know we're in a hurry to get on the air," I added, "and we can't afford to risk a long delay in court. So you're taking advantage of us. Just realize this—you're stealing from Almighty God, and nobody gets away with cheating *Him!*"

Nearly a year later the insurance company filed suit against a number of people to try to recover most of the company's losses, but they got almost nothing for their trouble.

As I reflect on all this today, I have come to this realization: The great Creator of the heavens and the earth seems to enjoy allowing Satan to do his worst, and then Almighty God glorifies Himself by bringing victory out of apparent defeat. The Book of Job is a perfect example of this remarkable spiritual phenomenon.

Although we were cheated out of $100,000, it didn't seem to bother the Lord in the least.

Wayne and Al, the *PTL Club's* engineers, made a profound observation: "Everything is going more smoothly the second time."

The soot from the fire and the extinguishers, however, presented a continuing problem because it got into every nook and cranny of the electronic gear that had been unpacked. Until the day of this writing 20 years later, the equipment has suffered from occasional problems as a result. Thankfully, a significant amount of the new equipment had not been unpacked before the fire occurred.

We simply backed up and started again.

When Gale Brooks, whom Bill Freeman had known at CBN, applied for a job, we hired her. Skilled in many areas, Gale—like Bill, Oleen, and me—wore several hats.

Gale was adamant about one point: "We cannot be all Christian in our programing," she told us repeatedly.

Pat Robertson had adopted the concept of the "family station," which intersperses Christian and secular programing. Pat was of the opinion that unbelievers wouldn't watch an all-Christian station, and Gale agreed strongly with Pat.

Norma's vision had been for an all-Christian station, but Gale was arguing quite persuasively for the family station concept. I was weakening in my resolve. *After all*, I told myself, *Pat Robertson knows more about Christian television than I do.*

One morning Gale came to work with the strangest look on her face. She gathered Bill, Oleen, and me together.

"I have something to tell you," she announced with some emotion. "I had a dream last night. Jesus appeared in my dream and told me that WPCB-TV was to be *all* Christian!"

We were amazed—and delighted. The Lord had intervened again! And so it has been to this day.

"So how *will* we program WPCB-TV?" we asked one another.

Destruction, Duplicity—and a Deep Freeze

From left to right: Russ, Wayne Fast, Bill Freeman, Gale Brooks (with the Porta-Jon in the background).

One day Oleen had a sudden vision from the Lord. She saw a picture of three E's: Entertainment, Evangelism, Edification. We were to *entertain*...in order to *evangelize*...in order to *edify*.

I didn't understand the concept then, but 20 years have demonstrated its effectiveness. The three E's still guide our programing philosophy.

The money, however, remained in extremely short supply. Many times Bill Freeman, Oleen Eagle, Gale Brooks, and I had to wait for our paychecks. Our suppliers often wouldn't sell us anything unless we gave them full payment in advance.

Many vendors were demanding overdue payments, and we didn't have enough money. This really troubled us, for, as Oleen says, "It profanes the name of the Lord." Somehow we managed to stagger along.

Pat Robertson graciously gave us a gift of $25,000, with a promise of another $25,000 later. What a godsend! Every day we'd gather for prayer, holding hands in a circle, and thank God for the money to make our paychecks.

Faith Works

Dear Eleanor Blazevich, who lives close to WPCB-TV, invited us for dinner time after time. Her husband Joe never knew how many people would be crammed around their dinner table when he arrived home from work. Their home was a haven of warmth and joy through some dark days.

The old house trailer continued to provide all our office space—and an opportunity for genuine close fellowship! With no indoor plumbing on the hill for more than a year, we used an outside Porta-Jon. In mild weather we didn't mind so much, but the winter of 1978-79 was an experience.

The women found a "picnic commode" and taped a big sign on the door saying "Ladies ONLY!" All of us fellows had to go outside in the cold and snowy weather.

After we went on the air, the Porta-Jon continued to serve us for a time. At that point, we installed an inside light for

The directors at the Rally. From left to right: Russ, Norma, Oleen Eagle, Ernie Frederick, Jim Laine (in background), Harold McKam-

nighttime use—until we noticed that it silhouetted everything inside the plastic Porta-Jon. The light was quickly replaced by a flashlight! The completion of indoor plumbing in a second house trailer was cause for great celebration.

Finally we could see a target date: Easter Sunday afternoon, April 15, 1979. "As Jesus was raised from the dead on that day, so will be WPCB-TV, Channel 40," we told one another. We set 2:00 p.m. as the time to go on the air.

Surely Satan has fired his last cannon, I thought. But I was wrong. He had reserved additional salvoes for us, and targeting technical equipment seemed to be his favorite dirty trick.

Our engineers continued to work toward the new target date. If I noticed that Al McCarty and Wayne and Steve were having a problem, I would ask, "Do you guys need prayer?"

Al would smile every time and say, "God's got everything under control." And the problem would always be resolved.

I don't know how many times I heard Al say those five words, "God's got everything under control."

The engineering team we had hired to "pull proof of performance" had the transmitter running, with color bars showing, while they were testing all the equipment.

During the test, Christians all over the Pittsburgh viewing area excitedly watched the color bars for hours. It was a time of praise for every viewer. Color bars, however, aren't enough to meet the Federal Communications Commission's rigid standards for broadcasting.

The engineers worked until 2:00 a.m. Friday night. Exhausted, they decided to let the transmitter run while they went to their motel for a few hours' sleep. They planned to return at 8:00 a.m. Saturday with a full day of work ahead of them.

Faith Works

That Saturday—the day before Easter—I was in Philadelphia on a ministry trip. My plan was to arrive home late that night, just hours before the on-air time of 2:00 p.m. Sunday. As a result, I missed the devil's next blast.

Saturday morning dawned clear and cold, bringing the final hard freeze of the winter season, with the temperature dropping well down into the 20's. On Friday, the engineers had been using water instead of antifreeze to test the cooling lines of the transmitter. They were planning to put antifreeze in the cooling lines after all the plumbing leaks were repaired.

At 7:00 a.m. Saturday, the coldest moment of the day, the electric power inexplicably went off. No storm, no damage to power lines, no good reason at all—the electricity from the local electric company just went off!

Our transmitter stopped running, and by the time the engineers arrived at 8:00 a.m., streams of water were squirting out all sides of the heat exchangers. The water had frozen and blown holes throughout those cooling units!

The engineers shuddered when they saw the damage.

George Kemp came up and surveyed the situation. "We can't go on the air without cooling units," the engineers told George.

He called Harold McKamish, who loaded one of the heat exchangers into his truck and then drove all over Pittsburgh looking for someone to solder the holes on Saturday afternoon.

After about two-thirds of the holes were temporarily fixed, the engineers cut off the water supply to the rest of the cooling units. Since it was so early in the spring, the engineers decided that the partially repaired unit could handle the job until a permanent replacement could be purchased and installed.

Destruction, Duplicity—and a Deep Freeze

By nightfall the transmitter was working, and the engineers notified the FCC as required. We were ready for Easter Sunday!

Henry Harrison, co-host of the *PTL Club*, was coming to celebrate with us. Incidentally, I cannot say too much about Jim Bakker's liberality in helping us, again and again, as he graciously allowed Henry to participate with us.

Norma and I—along with our two youngest sons, Harold and John, who had been trained to operate the cameras—arrived at the station about 10:00 a.m. My heart sank when I noticed all the engineers huddled in front of the "exciter," that delicate frequency-sensitive piece of gear that creates the actual signal.

"What's wrong?" I asked Al McCarty, expecting to hear, "God's got everything under control."

Instead, Al looked troubled, saying with an urgency in his voice, "Pray!" I had never heard that from Al before; he seemed alarmed.

We're covered, I thought. After all, we had the extra exciter that went through the fire. It was dirty, but still in working condition.

When the engineers pulled the new exciter out and replaced it with the original one, it wouldn't work either! This went on for several hours as they alternated the exciters.

At last they called the chief engineer from Channel 22 (Julian Smith's station), where they had the same type of transmitter and exciter. He came over immediately, but neither exciter would work for him either.

The target time of 2:00 p.m. came and went. The largest cable system in the area was waiting for us to go on air, and people all over the Pittsburgh viewing area wondered where we were. Many viewers eventually became discouraged, turned off their television sets, and did other activities.

Norma said, "We've got to praise the Lord!" And we did; in fact, we got a little wild in that tiny studio as we sang and rejoiced, thanking God for the miracle we knew He was about to perform.

We were all praying earnestly while the engineers kept switching exciters, testing this and that. Finally, after 3:00 p.m., for no apparent reason, one of the exciters began functioning properly!

Satan, "the prince of the power of the air," had performed one more nasty trick to keep us from our mission to clean up air pollution. We were invading his territory—the airwaves!

Announcing . . .

Western Pennsylvania's Own
Christian Television Station!
WPCB-TV
Channel 40

. . . going on the air

EASTER SUNDAY,
APRIL 15, 1979

Life Begins at 40

. . . proclaiming the Good News of Jesus Christ
. . . serving the local church
. . . building up the Body of Christ

For free program schedule write or phone:
WESTERN PENNSYLVANIA CHRISTIAN BROADCASTING COMPANY
Box 17220, Pittsburgh, PA 15235
(412) 824-3930

Chapter 6

On—and Off—the Air

At precisely 3:30 p.m., Easter Sunday, April 15, 1979, WPCB-TV, Channel 40, went on the air for Jesus!

I was pleased to present a new Christian television station to the Greater Pittsburgh community. Henry and Susan Harrison of the *PTL Club* were there—Susan on the prayer phones and Henry on camera with me.

"Phone in and give us the name of your community," we invited viewers. "We'd like to know who's out there watching!" The calls came from miles around, and within hours we were celebrating the first salvation on WPCB-TV.

Pat Robertson phoned and offered his congratulations on the air. That first evening, at 7:30 p.m. on Easter Sunday, *The 700 Club* was shown on WPCB-TV, precisely as I had been claiming publicly for so long. And *The 700 Club* has been aired on WPCB-TV for these 20 years.

A favorite saying of mine is one that the dean of our seminary used to quote: "Let the life you live make liars out of your accusers." God is indeed our Vindication!

A number of prominent local Christians came on the air to offer their congratulations. Until the time for *The 700 Club,* we were live all that first afternoon. Our Board of Directors and their spouses manned the prayer phones for several hours.

Pastor Jim Laine had brought two handkerchiefs for Norma and me to use, but we didn't need them. We were "numb," having long since shed all our tears for WPCB-TV. Jim had to use one of the handkerchiefs himself!

One note of sadness, however, pervaded that day. Norma's Dad, who had taught science for years in public school, would have loved to have been present, but he had died of cancer just two months earlier.

The fulfillment of this vision was a triumph involving many of God's people working together, all with singleness of purpose. To this day nothing has changed.

The next day, after I had left home for the station, Norma received a phone call. It was the agnostic station director from Channel 53, the man who had accused me of playing a cruel game and raising money for an impossibility. He was crying.

"I didn't believe you could do it!" he sobbed. "And your picture is better than ours was when we first went on the air!"

From time to time people ask me to counsel them about starting a Christian television station. Few of these eager Christians ever persist.

Until Owen Carr put WCFC-TV, Channel 38, on the air in Chicago, there had been a procession of abortive attempts at Christian television in Chicago. Each excited pioneer stopped at the point where the fire got too hot for him. Owen persisted, however, and Channel 38 was on the air for Jesus for nearly 25 years.

I always have three questions to ask everyone who tells me he wants to build a station:

1. Did God tell you to build a Christian television station?
2. Will you be truly ecumenical?
3. Are you willing to walk on the water?

Concerning point three: Since the attacks will be supernatural, our work must also involve the supernatural; we *must* expect the miraculous.

The attacks during those nine horror-packed years of struggle had been so severe against Norma and me that they could have destroyed our health or perhaps even killed one of us.

Shortly after Channel 40 went on the air, we were having one of our daily 2:00 p.m. prayer meetings. A visiting evangelist, Manasseh Mankuleiyo of Kenya, who knew none of our

Manasseh Mankuleiyo of Kenya, Africa.

history, seized my right hand and Norma's left hand and began to prophesy. The Lord commended us for our faithfulness, then said, through the evangelist, "So I have given you both your *health* as a prize of war!"

Norma and I looked at each other, realizing in that moment that, indeed, we were both in good health! Another great excuse to praise the Lord!

Helen Mierski, Bill Bair, and Russ on *Getting Together*.

I have always felt that Christians should work together, making me what some people humorously call an "ecumaniac." I believe it is the will of God to cooperate; God honors it.

In 1979, when we first went on the air, CBN had several morning programs on Channel 53. For that reason, we decided to begin our broadcast day at 2:00 p.m. and continue until early morning. That made us Pittsburgh's first all-night television station. After CBN dropped all their programs on Channel 53 except *The 700 Club,* we began to program 24 hours each day.

On—and Off—the Air

We did not have to wait long to learn that the ministry was having an immediate effect. Norma received a letter from a Christian lady shortly after we went on the air. She told Norma how her children were grown and married and settled elsewhere. Then her husband died, and she was very lonely. Soon this lady discovered WPCB-TV and rejoiced: "Now I have a family again; you're in my living room every evening."

Also, an elderly woman was praying for her husband's salvation. She described him as "a good man," but one who had never committed his life to Jesus. Then WPCB-TV came on the air and—during one of our first days as we were praying "the sinner's prayer" on *Getting Together*—this man prayed with me. Two weeks later he "graduated"!

"I am so thankful to God for a Christian station," she wrote. "My husband was saved just in time!"

"How soon can we have a telethon?" I asked Bill and Gale. After all, they were our only Christian television veterans.

Chico Holiday singing during a 1979 telethon. (Randy Estelle is in the background.)

"Three months, minimum! People have to get to know us first."

"But we can't wait! We're broke!" So we held our first telethon after only two months. The goal was minimal—only $30,000—and we didn't even come close to making it.

We did, however, have one cause for celebration: our first $100 pledge! Everybody in the studio cheered when it was read on the air.

Pat Robertson's second gift of $25,000 arrived about this time; otherwise, we would not have survived.

Over the next few years, when we'd get in serious trouble, I would phone CBN, and Pat would send an occasional $5,000 or $10,000 gift. Again and again God used Pat Robertson's special friendship to lift us out of near-disaster.

Western Pennsylvania's hills make it essential for any television signal to be carried on every cable system. That situation created a satanic warfare that we had not anticipated.

Although all the cable systems in the area were required by law to carry WPCB-TV, some took a long time to get us on their systems. A very few stubbornly fought us, teaching us how bitterly some people hate God.

One cable system owner—who claimed to be an atheist—went to *great* expense to separate the small portion of his cable system within the area of mandatory carriage to avoid the legal requirement of carrying Channel 40 on the greater part of his system. He wasted many thousands of dollars merely out of pride. Now that he is dead and it is too late for him, he is no longer an atheist.

On—and Off—the Air

Other cable systems pulled dirty tricks. In Pittsburgh there are four VHF television stations, broadcasting on channels 2, 4, 11, and 13. Those are the four cable channels where a "ghost" *live* signal interferes with the cable system. As a result, the cable companies normally use those four "garbage" channels for announcements, promotional items, etc. Except for us. Several of the cable companies placed WPCB-TV—and no other station, just the Christian station—on one of those channels.

The FCC requires cable systems to deliver a "clean" signal, but if the customers don't complain to the cable company, they don't do anything about it. The viewers often think that the poor picture is our station's fault. We realized that many would-be supporters were not receiving a clear picture of WPCB-TV for that reason.

"I can't get Channel 40 on my little portable television set," my secretary complained to me one day. "But I can watch all the other Pittsburgh stations."

"Why don't you lay hands on your set and pray," I suggested.

"Do you think that will work?" she wondered.

"Well, I heard about a Roman Catholic convent that was located about 30 miles from the nearest Christian television station," I explained. "The nuns wanted to watch the 3:00 p.m. Bible study program, but the picture was much too snowy. In faith they gathered around, laying their hands on the television set, and prayed that the Spirit of God would bring in a clear signal. Thereafter the nuns were able to join the larger Christian community in Bible study—and with a clear picture."

Nancy did as I suggested, but the Channel 40 signal still would not come through.

Then one day Nancy excitedly came into my office. "I was dusting my furniture and accidentally knocked the television set against the wall. But I caught it before it hit the floor," she related. "After it was back on the stand, I turned it on to see if it still worked."

"Did it?"

"Yes! But now I can't get any station *except* ours!"

W e were always behind in our finances.

The local power company somehow made an error in our electric bill during that first year and, while we waited for them to get the billing corrected, we fell ten months behind!

One day someone from the electric company phoned. "We are going to pull the plug if you don't pay at least $36,000 immediately!"

Edwin Louis Cole, who helped with the financial emergency for the electric bill.

On—and Off—the Air

That evening Ed Cole and George Otis Sr. were scheduled to be on *Getting Together*.

When Ed walked in the studio, he immediately asked, "What's wrong, Russ? Is something troubling you?"

I didn't realize my face was mirroring the problem. "We need $36,000 right away," I told him.

"Just a moment," he said and he got in a huddle with George.

The two men came back triumphantly: "We're going to raise that $36,000 tonight!"

They had 90 minutes, and they very nearly did it—almost, but not quite. After George read the amount of one significant pledge on the air, he slapped it with his other hand in front of the camera, and shouted, "So there!" And named the electric company!

Oh no, George! I thought. *Don't stir up the electric company against us! We have enough problems!* My fears were unfounded, and soon the bill was totally paid off.

Over the years, our viewers have always responded whenever we have been in a serious financial bind. They begin praying and giving!

One of our long-time employees commented, "With all the financial miracles God has accomplished for this ministry, the greatest miracle is that I never missed a single paycheck!"

WPCB-TV desperately needed a van, but there was no money to pay for one. As usual, we went to prayer and began asking God to give us a van.

During this time, Gale Brooks came to me and asked, "Russ, would you drive me to my mother's home near Clarion, Pennsylvania?"

I agreed. Along the way, we stopped at her cousin's auto body shop. When we were introduced, I thought, *This guy sure looks depressed about something.*

A few minutes later Gale took me aside. "My cousin went to the doctor today. His test results indicate that his physical condition is fatal."

This man had not been interested in the gospel before, but I had an open door that afternoon, and he accepted Jesus. I then laid my hands on him and prayed for healing.

Within minutes he said, "I feel like a new man; I'm healed!"

Gale's cousin was so grateful that he asked, "Is there anything WPCB-TV needs?"

Gale pointed toward a nice van.

WPCB-TV's "miracle" van and early trailer.

"That van was in a wreck, but I got it for a junk price and fixed it up," he explained. "You can have it for the cash I paid for it."

The Lord seems to have no limit to the methods He uses to provide for this ministry!

Our building was so tiny that the entire television station was packed into a 24-foot by 48-foot space. If the director called for a "wide" shot of the talk set, the cameraman had to back into the prayer partners' desk and lean backward over the telephones with the camera handles pressed against his body.

Sometimes it was so funny that I could hardly refrain from laughing. How comical to see a prayer partner with his or her eyes closed in prayer suddenly pressed in the forehead by a cameraman leaning as far back as possible!

Each afternoon the engineer had to work several hours just to get our two cheap cameras balanced enough to make acceptable pictures. When a camera would go out of balance during *Getting Together,* the engineer would run in and smack the camera—hard!—and it usually worked.

Every afternoon we met for prayer in that tiny studio, where we would hold hands and thank the Lord for enough money to make the next payroll—as well as an "impossible" dream of a new studio.

Our good friend from El Paso, Alex Blomerth, who has constructed and maintained countless Christian radio and television stations, was visiting one day. He joined the prayer meeting and afterward commented, "I have never found such faith at a Christian station. I know God's going to give you that new studio!"

We had been given a small, outdated mobile TV unit that we used for production control for some months because our facility was so cramped. Every day we hooked it up—outside the building—and each night we took it apart.

Finding qualified—and responsible—employees presented a constant dilemma.

Bill and Marilyn Bair of the Bair Foundation helping on the phones.

We had a hippie master-control operator part-time on Sunday evenings. Our third Sunday on the air he fell asleep with his face on the control panel. The 7:00 p.m. program tape ran out at 7:30, and he slept through a half-hour of blank "air." We were on the air, but nothing was being broadcast. At 8:00 p.m., he woke up in time to start the scheduled videotape. That ended his career in Christian television.

Our efforts often appeared amateurish, and many people—including some of the staff—thought we would not last through the year. Sometimes, however, the power of God would fall, and all our problems would be forgotten.

One evening the power fell on Norma, and many people at home were touched by the healing power of the Holy Spirit. Our accountant phoned his wife to tell her to turn on the TV

Father Michael Scanlan, president of the Franciscan University, Steubenville, Ohio, Bill Freeman, and Russ, 1979.

quickly, but she couldn't talk; she was already in tears from watching that anointed program.

J esse Curry, a very stubborn yet quite delightful man in his 70's, had been climbing where only a younger man should have been working, and he fell. At the hospital the X-rays showed a clear break in the pelvic bone.

"You must be in a body cast for a number of weeks in order for the pelvic bone to heal," the doctor told him.

"Nope!" responded Jesse. "Send me home! Jesus is going to heal me!"

The doctor was disgusted—with good reason—but he could do nothing.

Jesse was in great pain, but he crawled up on his living room couch and began watching WPCB-TV, which had just recently gone on the air. He lay there for two weeks, watching our station for hours at a time and stoically putting up with his pain.

One evening on *Getting Together* Norma saw a vision. She said, "There's a man who fell and broke his pelvic bone. The break looks like this." And she traced a crooked line with her finger in the air.

Suddenly the power of God surged through Jesse's body, and he jumped off the couch, totally healed!

Thereafter Jesse called Norma "my girlfriend," and he would kiss her every time they met.

Jesse lived ten more very interesting years, and later died of cancer at home, refusing all medical care other than pain killers.

Jesse's wife, Mercer, was the most remarkable black woman I've ever known. Mercer was, until she "graduated" in 1997 at the age of 86, our most powerful prayer warrior. We always knew that when Mercer Curry was praying for us, everything would work out okay.

Mercer was an evangelist and a prophetess. Having preached and prophesied over much of the earth—praying with prominent people in many lands—we felt quite privileged to know that her contribution would be arriving faithfully every month. Mercer was afraid of no one.

Jesse and Mercer's son, Jerry, is today a retired army general—and at one time the highest-ranking black officer in the U.S. Army. On one of his visits to his family, Mercer asked her general-son, "How would you like to be as good a Christian as you think you are?"

Her boldness piqued Jerry's interest, and that day he was baptized in the Holy Spirit. Suddenly General Jerry Curry became as bold for the Lord as his mother, and his witness made quite an impact in the Pentagon. In fact, Mercer preached there a number of times, and the military brass loved her.

Two weeks before she died, Mercer had been on a preaching tour of Finland. We lost a very special saint of God when Mercer Curry went to be with the Lord.

"This prayer phone is still not working," Steve Totin said.

Although a technician from the phone company had checked it out, he couldn't get the phone to work. Steve took the handset off the receiver and laid it on the desk. Normally, when the prayer partners are finished for the evening, they take all the handsets off the receivers.

That evening, as I was talking to a guest after *Getting Together* had ended, a phone started ringing. I assumed that one of the prayer partners had absentmindedly left a handset on the receiver.

I called to Steve Totin, "Could you answer the phone?"

Steve located the ringing phone. It was the one that was out of order! But that was impossible; it couldn't have been ringing. Not only was it out of order, it was also off the receiver! Yet it was ringing! Steve picked it up and answered hesitantly.

A man's voice asked plaintively, "Could you please tell me how I can be born again?"

Another miracle! After the caller had accepted Jesus, Steve checked the phone, but it was dead once again! The Lord had used an out-of-service phone miraculously! What love God demonstrated that evening! We all learned a vital lesson: Every single soul is important to God!

One summer evening the electric power went off due to a thunderstorm. Everything stopped except the prayer phones. "Ma Bell" could always be depended upon. The prayer phones kept ringing in spite of the fact that we were off the air and without lights. In the dark, the prayer partners couldn't see to quote scripture or to write down the prayer requests.

To get light, we opened the door to the studio, drove a car around to the back of the building, and aimed it at the door— and the counselors wrote with the help of the headlights. So the ministry continued.

Other television stations have large diesel generators for emergency power, but 20 years later, we still are unable to afford a generator, although we plan to purchase one soon

Whenever we were off the air due to a thunderstorm, the problem could usually be traced to the electric company. Channel 40 is located at the end of the power line and several miles from the substation—an *old* facility that the electric company has refused to improve even though we are one of their best customers.

Three times in our early days the huge klystron tubes blew. Nobody knew why; we didn't have a chief engineer to research the problem.

At that time, the tubes cost $18,000 each. (Today they cost in excess of $50,000.) As God would have it, they were leased, and the manufacturer had to replace them.

After three blown tubes, the manufacturer said, "No more! From now on, *you* purchase the tubes."

We found a chief engineer, and he and the other engineers detected and repaired the cause of the damage.

We also had a gas leak in the transmission line, which the tower repair company couldn't locate for years. We had to buy countless tanks of nitrogen gas to maintain the proper pressure in the 800-foot transmission line.

Russ teaching during an early telethon.

At times, we were off the air for long periods—even up to three days. When viewers would call their cable companies, wondering what was wrong with WPCB-TV, the cable people would sometimes say, "I think they're out of business." As a result, many Christians didn't know whether to support us or not.

The devil never gave up.

One day, after we had been knocked off the air again, one of our engineers told me, "I ordered the replacement equipment, and it will arrive by Federal Express tomorrow morning."

"It won't make it," I said. "I know what the devil's up to."

"No," he insisted. "Federal Express will have it here in the morning. Guaranteed!"

It arrived a day late, as I knew it would. So we were off the air an extra day.

Christian television is simply continual warfare—spiritual warfare. I was once again reminded of Pat Robertson's warning: "It's like walking into a blizzard. It can't stop you, but you must keep walking."

Chapter 7

A "Family" of Experts

"**L**ord, we desperately need another engineer!" That had become my repeated cry during the staff prayer meetings.

One day we received a call: "This is Gary Stewart, and I live in West Virginia. I heard you were looking for an engineer."

To minimize his expenses, Gary usually brought a large bag of sandwiches to work. When they were gone at the end of the week, he refused any offers of food.

"Gary, let me buy you dinner," I suggested. "It's a long ride back to West Virginia."

"No thanks," he always politely declined. "I'll eat when I get home."

As I got to know Gary, I learned that he had grown up in Connecticut, where he had acquired politically liberal ideas. "I considered Southerners to be a bunch of Nazi-type rednecks," he told me.

"Why did you move to West Virginia?" I quizzed Gary.

"My goal was to instigate political change," he explained, "but I didn't want to get too far south and be lynched by an angry mob of skinheads!"

"How did you get saved?" I asked.

"I have always been interested in economics, so I began listening to an economics program on a local Christian radio station. After the program ended, my wife Jean would keep listening. She heard the gospel preached and accepted Jesus as her Savior."

"What did you think of that?"

"I was really confused," Gary told me. "But Jean challenged me to listen, and I finally committed my life to Jesus Christ, too."

"What about your liberal ideas?" I wondered. "After all, the Holy Spirit is the Spirit of Truth."

Gary and Jean Stewart.

A "Family" of Experts

"That's right," Gary agreed. "My left-wing politics died immediately, and I promptly became a conservative political activist—and not because any human being told me to!"

Later Gary Stewart moved to Pittsburgh to work full-time at Channel 40, where he has been a most valued and dependable engineer for nearly 20 years. His wife Jean faithfully volunteered at the station until she took a position teaching school.

Part of Gary's job involves representing Cornerstone with the cable systems, which he does quite capably. He also has provided stability in the engineering department during the times we have changed chief engineers.

Another engineer, Marty Gutwerk, came to work for us that first summer. Marty, a great troubleshooter, could always find the problem when something went wrong.

Marty and his wife Josie lived in a mobile home, which they parked on our hill. What a blessing it was to have them living on the property! Whenever we needed more prayer partners, Josie was usually willing to help—even when it was inconvenient for her.

One weekend Josie heard Marty yell, "Fire!"

When she ran outside, Josie saw Marty with a fire extinguisher putting out flames that were shooting out from beneath our accounting trailer.

Since it was a weekend, all our financial records would have gone up in smoke without his intervention. Praise the Lord!

Today Josie still works part-time for Cornerstone TeleVision.

S lowly a number of local pastors became interested and supportive of the television ministry. Those congregations that supported us liberally usually found themselves prospering, too.

Our goal has always been to support the local church, and we encourage viewers to attend Bible-teaching, evangelical congregations near where they live.

For years, we sent the names of people saved through the television ministry to churches in their local areas. Only a few pastors, however, followed up on discipling these new believers.

Some pastors realized that television is the greatest tool for effective evangelism available to Christians today. A few local churches have televised their services on WPCB-TV through the years, but only one, Central Baptist Church of Pittsburgh, has maintained this commitment continuously for more than 15 years.

Their late pastor, Dr. Isaac Green—with whom I enjoyed a precious relationship—was a true visionary. The current pastor,

Dr. Isaac Green presenting a gift during a telethon.

Victor Grigsby, has continued the telecast. His excellent preaching has resulted in a growing congregation with new believers added to the Kingdom weekly.

Our station's association with Central Baptist Church has been a tremendous blessing to us as well. A number of Central's members volunteer faithfully on the phones during every telethon.

Through the years God has blessed those who bless this ministry. We claim for ourselves—and for our supporters—the blessing of Abraham: "I will bless those who bless you, and him who curses you I will curse" (Genesis 12:3a). This scripture is the privilege of every one who has been "born of the Spirit" (see John 3:5).

I n April 1979, after two weeks on the air, Oleen Eagle approached Bill Freeman and me with a solution to our disorganized videotape trailer.

"My nephew, David Skeba, is an ordained minister," she began. "His heart is really in the pastorate, but most congregations want a married pastor. He has a temporary job now, but he is a very organized person who could get our tape library in shape."

"Great!" Bill and I replied.

At first David wasn't interested, but—as a favor to his aunt—he agreed to work for three months. Soon we were actually able to locate tapes in the newly organized Programing Department.

The three months came and went, and David slowly came to realize: "Hey, I am a pastor after all. Through television programing I am ministering to the Greater Pittsburgh community."

Hiring David Skeba was one of the best moves we ever made. Today David is our Vice President and Director of Programing.

About the same time David came on board, Oleen's good friend, Sister Angela, phoned from California. "I need a temporary place to stay," she told Oleen. "I'm leaving the convent, and I was wondering if I could visit with you for awhile."

"Of course," Oleen replied.

Oleen brought Mary Anne (Sister Angela's given name) to the station where she quickly put her fine arts skill to work as our artist/set designer. Like most of us, she, too, wore many hats.

"Wouldn't David and Mary Anne make a nice couple?" we all told one another. After all, they were both past 30.

In spite of our matchmaking attempts, neither seemed interested in the other. Then the Great Matchmaker got involved, and the Holy Spirit began to draw David and Mary Anne together. Before I knew it, I was performing their wedding ceremony! Their romance had all the marks of a divine appointment.

Hardworking and productive, David has put together what we think is the best line-up of Christian programs of any Christian station in the world.

Mary Anne, with no formal training, has developed into a very skilled set designer. Not only has she designed all our sets elegantly

Mary Anne and David Skeba.

and inexpensively, she has also helped a number of other ministries. One of her budget-priced sets won the Silver Award at a national contest in Las Vegas.

David and Mary Anne Skeba are two of God's gifts to this ministry.

Before he graduated from high school, our son Paul had already decided to study television production. His choice had nothing to do with the fact that we were building a television station.

"I want to work in secular network television," he told us during his senior year at Oral Roberts University, where he was majoring in telecommunications.

One evening—shortly after WPCB-TV went on the air—the Lord spoke to Paul, telling him to go home and work for his dad. Paul resisted. Unable to sleep, he walked the streets of Tulsa all night, kicking the gravel and talking to the Lord.

The next day Paul phoned home. "Have you and Dad been praying that I would come home to work with you?" he asked his mom.

Norma answered truthfully, "We've been praying that God would send the people He wants here."

"Well, I'm supposed to be one of them."

Paul decided obedience to God was more important than his career plans.

At the time, however, Paul was early in his fifth year of college because he had been working long hours at the NBC affiliate station in Tulsa. He had stretched his courses and was still six credit hours short of the graduation requirements.

To his surprise the department head, Dr. Tom Durfey, agreed to let Paul come to Pittsburgh if he would do what is called an "independent study" that would count for his final six credits. Paul's graduation project—to put it bluntly—was "WPCB-TV before Paul" and "WPCB-TV after Paul." The improvements he made in our on-air look were quite noticeable!

The following January at the National Religious Broadcasters Convention, a man walked up to Norma and me. "Hi, I'm Tom Durfey," he said, "your son's dean at ORU." He then proceeded to tell us about Paul's skills and accomplishments. Finally, Tom concluded, "Paul can do anything in television that he sets his mind to do!"

I told him how pleased we were with Paul's performance at the station. "Paul helped to improve the operation at WPCB-TV and make it look respectable—all with the least and cheapest equipment possible."

Paul was opposed to working for us because he disliked being known as the boss' son. I didn't want him at the station for the same reason. Having seen many ministries deteriorate during the second generation, I have always questioned nepotism.

My fears were quickly put to rest. Paul loves to do television, but he has no interest in management whatsoever. His skills lie in the areas of producing and directing—and that's the way he likes it. Paul takes on some of our most difficult production jobs, and we always lean heavily on his judgment when it comes to purchasing new equipment.

I've occasionally told Paul, "You have your mother's skills." If Norma were 30 years younger, she'd be the very able producer of *Getting Together*. But Norma has always been a volunteer—our Number One Volunteer for these 20 years.

A "Family" of Experts

Like many of our other employees, God called Paul to work with us. Because of Paul's obedience, God gave him a very sweet, attractive wife, Faye, whom he met because Faye's brother-in-law worked for WPCB-TV.

Paul and Faye Bixler.

We were quickly becoming a television "family" in more ways than one!

"**W**e need a dependable person who will operate camera for minimum wage," Oleen told us.

"That's a lot to expect!" I joked.

One day Bob Taylor, a carpenter by trade, showed up after being recommended by one of our employees.

"Can you start right away?" he was asked.

"I guess so," Bob agreed and was immediately given a 15-minute lesson in how to run camera.

"Get ready!" the director ordered. "We're on the air!"

Suddenly a nervous Bob Taylor was standing behind a camera focused on the *Getting Together* set. The director was screaming at Bob to make certain moves.

"Zoom in!" the director shouted into Bob's headset as the singer for that evening's program began his song.

Bob did as instructed and got a close-up of the singer's mouth!

"Lose focus!" meant nothing to Bob, so the director yelled some more.

Finally, the song ended with a great picture of the man's hair!

As he became more proficient on camera, Bob told us, "I like it."

Bob Taylor setting up a microphone.

Our audio man, Ron King, was moonlighting for us each evening, driving nearly 100 miles round trip. But Ron was not a Christian. One evening I was preaching during *Getting Together* when, without warning, tears started flowing down Ron's cheeks. He started laughing uncontrollably—in the midst of all the tears. And Ron was promptly born again!

Finally, Ron King had to quit from sheer exhaustion.

A "Family" of Experts

Once again, someone said, "Maybe Bob Taylor can do audio."

Bob was tapped.

"That was worse than running camera the first time!" he said, still trembling from the experience.

During his first telethon, which is always fast-paced, Bob was so nervous that he broke out in hives. With experience, he developed into a superb audio man, and we have depended heavily upon him throughout the years.

Bob has a wonderful singing voice, and we should have realized that he would make a great audio man because of his feel for music.

Twenty years ago all television stations were required by the FCC to carry at least one daily (Monday through Friday) news program.

Bill Freeman, whose appealing voice has a remarkable range, took on the job of newscaster. With our limited budget, however, gathering news was not a priority for us. We merely leased a teletype machine.

When news time came at 5:00 p.m., Bill would "rip 'n' read," tearing off the teletyped pages and reading the news items.

Although we couldn't afford to focus on local news, the program came off rather well.

Television requires split-second teamwork—similar to a football team. During those early days, everybody wore several hats.

Just before 5:00 p.m. Barb Crowell jumped up from her secretary's desk, ran from the trailer to the tiny studio, and grabbed the camera for *The Five O'Clock News*. David Skeba dropped his videotapes and aimed the other camera at Bill Freeman. A number of our staff would suddenly appear to put together the mandatory news program.

When Bill Freeman left, Alan Jennings—now an NBC affiliate news reporter—also did a very professional job. Then the FCC began allowing the smaller stations to eliminate their news program, and we promptly—and gladly—dropped it.

The FCC, however, had another difficult requirement: public affairs programs.

Alan Jennings reading telethon pledges.

Oleen Eagle—who does quite well at matching people with jobs—recruited Marge Provan, a doctor's wife, who took on the entire responsibility of producer, guest coordinator, and on-air talent for *Focus on the Issues*. After ten years as a volunteer, Marge finally "ran out of steam."

A "Family" of Experts

Quite attractive and vivacious, Marge Provan was the first woman to be elected President of the Allegheny County Sportsmen's Association. Yes, Marge loves to hunt deer, and she's a pretty good shot with a target rifle, too.

Since Marge's resignation, Jerry Bowyer of the Allegheny Institute for Public Policy, a think-tank in the Pittsburgh area, has fulfilled the job admirably.

For two years, we televised the three programs in our little crackerbox studio: *Getting Together* (daily), *The Five O'Clock News* (daily), and *Focus on the Issues* (weekly, with taped repeats).

Stan Scott (and later his wife Loretta, too) came in from Wintersville, Ohio, to host the Wednesday evening *Getting Together* program.

A group of six television engineers from Erie, Pennsylvania, drove to Pittsburgh for a meeting of the Society of Broadcast Engineers. Two of the six were Christians, and they told the others, "We want to see the Christian station we've heard so much about."

As they toured our facility, one of them remarked, "There's not enough equipment here to call this a TV station!"

They were right.

"Most of what we have is secondhand," one of our engineers told them, "but we're still on the air 24 hours a day!"

As the staff prepared for *The Five O'Clock News,* all six engineers gathered around to watch. The four unbelievers snickered at our amateurish production.

Stan Scott reading a pledge, 1979.

When the time came for a ten-second video roll-in, the old videotape machine refused to "lock in." As the assistant director counted, "Six...five...four...," our engineer was still struggling to get it to lock in.

At two seconds, the engineer calmly stepped back, pointed his finger, and commanded, "In Jesus' name, lock in!"

Precisely after the voice counted "one," the VTR locked in and the roll-in went smoothly. Then the machine died again at the end of the needed ten seconds.

The four unbelievers stared incredulously as our engineer went about his business as if nothing unusual had happened.

Years later, one of the Christian visitors described this delightful miracle and distributed the story on the Internet. In his words, he wrote: "The operator never blinked. He rewound the tape, quickly set up the next segment, and moved on. It was just another average day at the station."

The visiting engineer concluded his Internet article: "...and they're still trying to find out if there's anything God can't do...even if you don't have all the stuff you need."

A "Family" of Experts

The FCC also has hiring requirements concerning women and minorities. We had enough women on staff, but I didn't know how to find minorities. Thankfully, God went ahead of us.

One Sunday evening I arrived at Christ Soul Saving Station, where I had been asked to preach. Afterward, the young organist introduced himself as Kevin Robinson and asked, "Do you need any additional employees?"

"We're always looking for qualified people," I told him.

"I just graduated from West Virginia University with a major in broadcast journalism," he stated.

"You did?" I was so excited, I almost floated! Not only was Kevin African-American, but he had the education we needed.

Kevin Robinson, Cindy Chester, Ralph Grimes, videotape operators, all long-time employees.

Kevin immediately started volunteering, and then went on salary in December of 1980. He has been with us ever since, working in several different capacities through the years.

115

In the beginning of our television ministry, my goal was to find someone competent to whom I could turn over the leadership of WPCB-TV after it was built.

"I enjoy teaching the Bible and writing books," I often told Norma, "so I don't want to spend the rest of my life in television."

God, however, had other plans. He has let me know again and again that I am not only to lead the ministry but also to be seen on our flagship program, *Getting Together*.

"But I'm so shy!" I told the Lord. Although I was comfortable in front of a congregation of flesh-and-blood people, I felt threatened by that cold camera lens.

My first appearances on television were awful! After some years, I was still intimidated by the cameras. Only gradually has God been setting me free from those fears.

Chapter 8

Operating a TV Station on Miracles

During our first year on the air, 1979, the Lord instructed me to organize and host a teaching seminar in Pittsburgh for budding Christian television stations. Just as we had needed help, I knew they did, too.

I phoned several Washington lawyers whom I knew to be Christians, asking for names and addresses of Christian applicants for station Construction Permits. I compiled quite a list and sent them information about the seminar.

People from across the nation came, including six Christian attorneys who practice before the FCC, as well as the Executive Director of the National Religious Broadcasters, Ben Armstrong, and his wife Ruth. Everyone was excited. Nearly 100 people showed up.

Several Christians who were about to give up on starting a Christian TV station went back home with renewed enthusiasm—and their stations are on the air to this day!

Faith Works

During one of our *Getting Together* programs that week, I interviewed Ben Armstrong.

Off camera, Ruth Armstrong was standing by Norma's chair, watching the interview. "Ruth, wouldn't you like to sit down?" Norma asked.

"No, thanks, I'd rather stand."

What Ruth didn't tell Norma was that she had a very severe back problem, and the ride from the airport to the station that day had been excruciating for her.

Suddenly, Norma stood up behind the camera and, motioning to me, put her hand behind her back and started bending over several times. At first I didn't understand her body language, but then I finally realized she was telling me that the Spirit was healing someone's *back*.

"Excuse me, Ben," I interrupted to mention the word of knowledge, "but God is healing someone's back."

Ruth Armstrong, who is rather fair-skinned, immediately turned crimson as the heat of the Holy Spirit went up and down her spine. At that moment, Ruth was instantly and permanently healed!

At the National Religious Broadcasters Convention two months later, Ruth Armstrong spotted me—and burst into tears. Later she saw Norma and fell on her shoulder, sobbing uncontrollably. "You don't know how many years I've suffered from pain in my back! Oh, I love you!"

At every convention for the next several years, Ruth would cry each time she saw us. Ben and Ruth have since appeared on *Getting Together* to give God the glory for His precious blessing for Ruth.

Norma and I love to praise the Lord for His glorious miracles.

Operating a TV Station on Miracles

Sadie was a retired Presbyterian missionary nurse, having spent most of her adult life in Thailand. Closely attached to the Thai royal family, Sadie's relationship had been almost like the one of Anna and the King of Siam in *The King and I*. In excellent health when she retired to her original home of Pittsburgh, Sadie began to develop an irregular heartbeat. Her doctor claimed that nothing could or should be done about the condition and that she should learn to live with it. As the irregular heartbeat worsened, Sadie began tripping over curbs and dropping teacups—to the point where she could hardly wash dishes.

One evening she turned on her television set, but nothing seemed to interest her. So Sadie returned to the kitchen to do some chores when she heard a voice say, "Channel 40!"

Oh, I don't want to listen to young people beating on drums! Sadie mistakenly thought.

"Channel 40!" repeated the voice. And she stopped what she was doing. Again she heard, "Channel 40!"

Intrigued, Sadie turned on the television set again. While waiting for the picture to appear, she heard Norma say, "God is healing somebody of a heart condition!"

Promptly I said authoritatively, "Place your hand on your heart and take a deep breath." She did, and the power of the Lord went through her body.

Severely frightened, Sadie quickly turned off her TV set. Puzzled, she walked around the apartment, trying to do everything she hadn't been able to do—with no problems whatever. And she wondered, "Who *were* those people?"

The next evening Sadie turned on Channel 40 to learn who we were. Sadie's niece was a friend of ours, so Leah brought her out to visit the station and meet us.

Sadie lived several more victorious years in great health. She died as the result of a stroke that was caused by extreme over-exertion, doing work no senior citizen should be doing. During those final years she was an even more effective witness for Jesus!

Praising the Lord. From left to right: Bill Freeman, Father Mike Salvagna, Norma, Dick Burns (United Methodist evangelist), Russ.

Our good friend Keith Houser was building a "family station," Channel 54, in Poughkeepsie, New York.

"Some of our programing will be Christian," Keith told us, "and it seems that the opposition to our station is demonic."

"Norma and I know all about that," I stated.

Norma decided her prayer group should drive to Poughkeepsie to pray around Keith's construction work. On the way down a long, lonely grade in the Pocono Mountains, the car's engine just stopped.

120

"What happened to the car?" one lady asked.

"I don't have any idea," the driver responded.

This struck one of the six women as funny, and soon the entire group was laughing hysterically. Several cars passed while the ladies were parked.

After the laughter subsided, Norma said, "Try the engine now." It started normally, and they drove on.

While the women were pondering this strange phenomenon, a policeman appeared by the side of the road, motioning frantically for them to stop. "There's a sheet of ice around this bend! I've already got two cars in the ditch!"

"That's why the engine so mysteriously stopped," one of the ladies said.

"The devil was trying to keep us from our mission in Poughkeepsie," another concluded as their laughter turned to praise.

In Poughkeepsie, they prayed over Channel 54's station/office complex. Then Keith Houser took them out to the tower site, which was almost completed.

The women all sensed the demonic activity, so they prayed earnestly there, then headed back to Pittsburgh.

The very next day Keith was inspecting the tower construction. As he was looking up, the foreman said, "Keith, come around to this side of the tower. You can get a better view of what's happening up there."

Keith walked around the tower just a few steps. Suddenly, a workman's wrench dropped 900 feet, split the ground, and buried itself. It struck precisely at the spot where Keith had been standing just seconds earlier!

The Super Seven's prayers probably saved Keith's life—and thus perhaps the whole project. Today Channel 54 is still spreading the gospel.

O ne day in 1980 I received a phone call from Steve Cancilla, a builder of churches. We had known each other for a number of years.

Even as a layman, Steve perceived his primary responsibility in life to be the spreading of the gospel at home and abroad.

"Russ," Steve began, "the Lord told me you need a new studio and that I am the person to build it."

"You're absolutely right," I responded. "We do indeed need a new studio—desperately—but we can't even pay our current bills, let alone build a new studio."

"That's okay," Steve said, "but remember, I'm to build your new studio. And just to prove that this is of the Lord, I'll be in on Monday to give you $25,000."

Just as he said, he came with a check—the largest contribution we had received from an individual.

I thanked Steve profusely, but added, "Steve, we really need this money to pay some old debts."

"I've given it to the Lord, Russ. Spend it as He leads."

We were able to pay off a number of bills with his generous gift.

Four days later one of the prayer partners received a call during our *Getting Together* program on Friday evening.

Operating a TV Station on Miracles

"This woman is hysterical," she said, "and she's demanding to speak to you." A soloist was singing on camera, so I took the call.

It was Steve Cancilla's wife, Rose. She screamed, "Steve had a heart attack while he was building a church in West Virginia, and the doctor says he can't live! Please pray! I'm on my way to the hospital!" And she hung up.

I had no idea where in West Virginia Steve had been working, and no way to find out.

We prayed, and I thought, *Well, there goes our new studio.*

We later learned that Steve had been building a church in northern West Virginia and was taken to a local hospital. As the doctor had predicted, Steve Cancilla died, and promptly found himself in heaven. So excited to be there, Steve bubbled, "I've got to see the Lord!"

As he was hurrying past the huge throngs of saints who were all praising Jesus, he recognized friends and relatives who had "graduated" earlier. Suddenly Steve stopped. "I can't stay here! I've got to build a television studio!"

Instantly his brother, who had died of cancer a couple of years earlier, stood before him. "You may go back now, Steve," he said. "Here is the key." And his brother placed something in Steve's hand. Before he had a moment to look down to his hand, Steve was awake in his hospital bed. It was Monday afternoon!

In a roomful of crying family and friends, Steve woke up laughing and praising Jesus! He began hugging and kissing everybody.

The doctor himself nearly had a heart attack! "Steve! You can't get out of bed! Three-fourths of your heart is damaged!" And the doctor gave him strict rules about diet and behavior.

"But," Steve told me later, "Jesus was talking to me at the same time. I knew I had a job to do."

Amazingly, Steve's blood pressure stabilized at 120/80 and his pulse at 72.

"Remember, Russ," Steve reminded me, "God wants me to build that studio! Let me know when you've got the money."

At that same time, Eleanor Clark of Fort Worth, Texas, had come to help the station with a desperately needed stewardship program. While she was in Pittsburgh assisting us, Eleanor received a phone call from a Christian man who wished to remain anonymous.

"I want to donate $150,000 for the express purpose of building a new studio for TV40," he stated, and then he gave her his name and phone number.

"I'll be in touch with you as soon as I return from a business trip to South Dakota for the Lowell Lundstrom ministry," she told him, and Eleanor put the information in her briefcase.

After flying from city to city in the Lundstroms' plane, Eleanor arrived in Watertown, South Dakota. When it came time to leave, she said stubbornly, without knowing why, "I'm not going to fly again today!" and refused to get back on the plane. In her haste, she forgot to retrieve her briefcase.

As the plane took off without Eleanor, it struck a high-tension line and exploded, crashing to the ground in flames. The pilot was killed instantly.

The fire from the crash had burned everything on board, including her briefcase. The keys in her case were twisted from the extreme heat, and the manila folders were destroyed—yet not one paper out of hundreds was burned except around the edges!

Operating a TV Station on Miracles

"That very day," Norma told us, "our prayer group had been praying for Eleanor's safety on all her plane trips!"

When the staff at TV40 learned of this series of miracles, we wondered: "What wonderful blessing does God have in store for us next?"

Very soon—September 17, 1980—we received the first installment on that $150,000 gift toward building a new studio.

Lieutenant Joe Blazevich of the Allegheny County Sheriff's Department (whose wife Eleanor had suggested the hill on which we built the station) had the privilege of carrying the first $25,000—in cash from our anonymous donor—onto the *Getting Together* set!

The first installment: $25,000 in silver coins. From left to right: Russ, Eleanor Clark, Oleen Eagle, Lt. Joe Blazevich, Bill Freeman.

Everyone except Steve Cancilla was surprised and thrilled. Steve had been expecting it.

"Can I build a studio for $150,000? I can do the shell. You'll have to raise the money for the insides." And he built it—in 11 months! Steve partitioned one end of the building for offices. By that time we had been working out of eight trailers and couldn't wait to move into our new addition.

Some months after the job was completed, Steve's heart stopped. This time he went joyously to see the Lord he had missed on his last trip heavenward. We'll never forget Steve Cancilla!

After Steve delivered us the shell of a building, our viewers eagerly got behind the project. As the builders completed the

Steve Cancilla explaining the new studio construction to Russ.

structure, money came rolling in to equip the studio and offices.

One Saturday, Harold McKamish organized a group of skilled volunteers to install the huge air-conditioning system. It was completed that very day.

Dale Bogard and friend. Dale volunteered countless hours building the new studio.

Before Steve Cancilla went to be with Jesus, the Lord had paid for the entire project. Many wonderful Christians contributed!

After exactly two years of televising from the "crackerbox," we moved into the new studio. Now we could begin to produce a number of other programs besides *Getting Together.*

We placed a large sign over the front door to the new building:

Thus says the Lord God: "Behold, I will lift up my hand to the nations, and raise my signal to the peoples"– Isaiah 49:22.

After serving the Lord in extremely cramped quarters in that first building, we wondered, "How will we ever fill a new 50-foot by 117-foot building?"

We didn't foresee how quickly we would grow. Within several years, we were full and overflowing again!

What a glorious opportunity God has given us to share the gospel of Jesus Christ!

A recent viewer survey revealed that 33 percent of those who watch Christian television stations are *not* believers. On occasion, we have been accused of "preaching to the choir," but this survey demonstrated the facts to be otherwise. Unbelievers *are* watching, and one by one, God grabs their hearts. At least they are being forced to make a decision—either for or against Jesus.

The key for this ministry is "the supernatural." The Holy Spirit is in charge, and we want to be led by the Spirit and empowered by the Spirit. Cornerstone TeleVision can reach those whom the local church is not reaching. We are already in the homes of people who would not be caught dead in church; or perhaps that's the only way they *would* be caught in church—dead.

Many testimonies over the years prove that God daily changes lives through the ministry of Christian television—sometimes in unexpected ways.

While at work in 1977, a Christian named Sam experienced a heart attack. He survived after being taken to the hospital.

One night three years later, in 1980, Sam and his wife Dorothy went to bed early. Suddenly Sam jumped out of bed and started praying excitedly. He ran his hand across his chest and down his left arm as he continued running up and down the hall, commanding, "Heart! Be healed, in Jesus' name!"

Dorothy cried desperately, "Lord, what can I do to help my husband?"

The Lord spoke gently in her heart, "You can turn on Channel 40." We were having a telethon, and it was getting late in the evening.

As her television set came on, the first words Dorothy heard me say were, "The Lord is healing somebody's heart, and you haven't even been diagnosed yet." While speaking this word of knowledge, I ran my hand across my chest and down my left arm just as Sam had done several minutes earlier.

Instantly, the pain left Sam's chest and arm, and nearly 20 years later, his heart still appears to be fine.

Sooner or later, everybody watches us. Some tune in to ridicule. Even then, such mockers usually sense that we do have the answers that they are searching for—or rather, *the* Answer.

One evening I was interviewing a local woman on *Getting Together*. The sister of my guest had begged her agnostic husband to watch: "After all, she's your sister-in-law!"

He agreed but did so while laughing and making wisecracks. Suddenly I looked into the camera: "There's a man watching, and you're mocking what God is doing here. But Jesus loves you anyhow; and just to prove it, He's healing your body right now!"

That man—our guest's brother-in-law—stood up, and the longtime pain in his back was *gone*! Now he really had a problem!

To me, it's simple: All of us in Christian ministries *must* recognize that the spiritual is greater than the physical. Producing

Christian radio and television programs can be so mundane, day after day, for years. After a while, it is easy to ignore the supernatural.

I am convinced that if we—as Christian broadcasters—do not learn to pray for, plant seed for, and expect the miraculous, we are simply not going to make it in the years just ahead of us.

One evening in the mid-80's, we invited Ruth Fisher, who formerly worked with Kathryn Kuhlman, to share her testimony on *Getting Together.* That night the power of God fell in the studio!

Ruth exclaimed on camera, "Where are the people? I've got to get my hands on the people!"

Ruth Fisher ministering to a hurting guest, with Russ.

Operating a TV Station on Miracles

"Consider it done, Ruth," I told her. "When can you come back?"

For her next visit, we filled the studio with needy folks.

God was faithful; He healed people for nearly an hour and a half! The healings took place not only in the studio, but also in homes.

Ruth, who is in her 80's and still loves to minister, comes several times each year, and the studio is full—or nearly so. In addition to dramatic healings, we always see a number of people saved. We have noticed that the anointing of the Spirit seems to last from 70 to 80 minutes every time she visits.

Of the countless exciting miracles, Joe Hysong's stands out.

The miracle service that touched Joe's life was broadcast live in the afternoon. During the program Ruth interrupted the flow with an unusual word directed toward the camera: "Sir, don't worry. You will not lose your leg." Then she went on with the service. This word seemed strange and quite out of place.

Joe Hysong lives in Wheeling, West Virginia, where he could not receive our signal. In 1983, he had broken his leg severely and had his *ninth* failed operation in 1984. The surgeon finally told Joe, "It's no use; we've got to take your leg off!"

Joe was sent to Pittsburgh's Presbyterian-University Hospital for the amputation. As a Christian, he'd been praying for a miracle, but none had materialized. To his delight, Joe found WPCB-TV on the television set in his hospital room, and he watched all evening.

During that time the anesthesiologist came in and explained, "Joe, I'm going to give you a shot now. It will put you to sleep. When you wake up tomorrow afternoon, the leg will have been amputated."

After the injection Joe went to sleep with the television set still on. Around 2:00 a.m., while we were *re-airing* the miracle service, Joe woke up—in spite of all the medication!

He heard Ruth Fisher say, "Sir, don't worry. You will not lose your leg." And then Joe went back to sleep.

In the morning, the surgeon was puzzled: "Something has happened!" Five or six doctors looked at his leg and decided that it didn't need to be amputated after all.

To this day, Joe walks normally on that leg—to the praise and glory of God!

Another outstanding miracle occurred to Shae, a 14-month-old infant in Pittsburgh's Children's Hospital, suffering with a four-centimeter tumor in her head. The tumor had grown so big that it was forcing Shae's eye out of its socket and turning it upward so much that the pupil could not be seen.

Shae's tumor had spread quickly down her spine, through her stomach, through her lungs—in fact, through much of her body. It was the fastest-growing type of juvenile cancer.

Frank, Shae's grandfather, was so touched by her illness that he got off by himself and committed his life to Jesus. Michele, Frank and Beverly's daughter, gave her life to Jesus in those moments also. The three of them were in the hospital watching Ruth Fisher on December 1, 1998, when Ruth abruptly announced, "Everybody stand up! Something remarkable is happening! A cancerous tumor is being healed, and it's not in the studio!"

Frank Skipper held up little Shae in front of the TV set in the hospital room. Beverly said later, "You could actually *feel* the power of the Holy Spirit filling the whole room!"

Suddenly Beverly began to notice the tumor shrinking. The eye slowly moved back into its socket as the tumor continued to shrivel. They promptly called WPCB-TV from the hospital room to report the miracle.

When the doctor came in, he thought it was the wrong baby. In amazement, he exclaimed, "A tumor never responds this way to a single chemotherapy treatment!"

The eye continued to improve, and several days later Shae was sent home. The rest of the cancer appeared to remain in Shae's body, but over a period of a few weeks, it all disappeared. Shae began to eat again, and promptly started gaining weight.

The Skippers were so grateful to God, to Ruth Fisher, and to Cornerstone TeleVision. "We want to help financially all we can," said Beverly.

The miracle services with Ruth Fisher and others are unique. Until Oral Roberts University built a television station in Tulsa, we were the only station to announce a live miracle service. Thus, if the Holy Spirit failed to show up, we would be in serious trouble.

During one miracle service, flames began shooting out of a lighting connection overhead. It was over *my* head, to be precise—and it was not Pentecostal tongues of fire!

This was *live* television, and Ruth Fisher and I had to continue talking, acting as if nothing were wrong. A slow shower of white powder was drifting down on our heads, and nobody in the studio was paying attention to what we were saying. All eyes in the audience were on the flames over our heads.

Ruth certainly showed her professionalism; she never once looked up. Suddenly two engineers appeared, running as fast as they could while carrying a long stepladder. They had to squeeze between a camera and the studio audience.

As the engineers finally got to the front with the ladder, Ruth and I gently moved to one side to give them room. At the same time, the cameramen moved with us so the viewers at home could not see all the frantic activity.

The ladder, however, had been positioned backwards, and the men had to hurry back out with it. When they finally got it turned around, the two men ran in with the ladder again, opened it up, and one went up and quickly disconnected the wires. It was "Keystone Kops" unrehearsed! We could hardly refrain from laughing.

In spite of that hilarious incident, miracles still occurred that day!

One evening during *Getting Together,* the Holy Spirit prompted me to speak out a word of knowledge about a healing for a liver. Nobody called or wrote to acknowledge the healing.

About six months later a key guest canceled, and we had to repeat the tape of an earlier program. The producer picked that very tape.

Meanwhile, Minnie, whose atheist husband wouldn't allow her to watch our station, was in the hospital. One of her joys there was to be able to view WPCB-TV. She heard me speak that word of knowledge about a liver being healed—given six months earlier—and the power of the Holy Spirit went through her body. She was healed!

Operating a TV Station on Miracles

The earlier tests had clearly shown three tumors on her liver, and when the surgeon operated, the tumors were gone! After six months on videotape, the anointing was still fresh! God had prepared that word and kept it until Minnie was in a place to receive it.

This phenomenon is not unusual. During a broadcast of *The 700 Club,* Pat Robertson had a word of knowledge for a child's healing. Later, the program was translated into Spanish, and Pat's interpreter repeated the word of knowledge in Spanish. When the program was aired six months later in Central America, a mother watched her little girl being healed of the specific illness Pat had described—right in front of her eyes!

Would that the Holy Spirit would do such miracles every day! Perhaps He does, and we just don't know it. If the results are not reported back to us, we cannot record them. We know, however, that the Holy Spirit is at work whether confirmation is received today or some day in the future. Whatever the situation, television was indeed created by God for very personal and powerful ministry.

Pat Robertson may be talking about politics on *The 700 Club* and then may easily move into the healing dimension on the same program. I really appreciate his ministry.

The Spirit of God told me years ago that *The 700 Club* is the most important program on television! That is quite a statement. Although no one is perfect and we all make mistakes, God continues to anoint and use Pat Robertson to bring the gospel to a lost and dying world through the ministry of *The 700 Club.*

Healing miracles are an important part of Christian television ministry. First Corinthians 12:9 (NKJ) notes, "to another gifts of healings," with *healings* in the plural. These "gifts of healings" work out in practical healing ministries for very specific illnesses, such as deafness, blindness, cancer, etc.

God has used me in healing many ailments and injuries, but a list of *back* healings would number in the thousands. I don't understand it; I just use it, to the glory of God. Years before WPCB-TV went on the air, I had realized that God had given me a gift of healing "backs"—spines, disks, back pain, etc. I even scheduled a special healing service on television for back ailments only, and we praised the Lord as He restored the backs of a studio filled with hurting people.

A lmost from the first day we went on the air, I seemed to have an awareness that someone was going to *die* in the studio during a *Getting Together* program. I knew that we should not be concerned but simply pray for the person, and he or she would be all right. That awareness came over me many times during the first five or ten years.

One evening we were honoring our telephone prayer partners, and the studio was crowded with these volunteers. Each person was given the opportunity to give his or her own brief personal testimony on camera. One extremely nervous woman with a heart condition had just testified.

A few moments later, as I went with the microphone to interview another prayer partner in the audience, I heard a loud noise behind me. Turning around, I saw the woman with the heart condition slumped down in her seat. She had turned ashen gray.

As God would have it, there was a nurse on each side of her. They both took her pulse and shook their heads.

With no prompting, our well-trained, faithful prayer partners began to pray as one person. By the time the rescue squad arrived, the woman appeared to be normal. All this took place during live television!

The prayer partner, however, had no memory of anything that had occurred to her, and she has consistently maintained that she didn't die. But all of us around her knew she was dead; there was no sign of life for several minutes.

After that evening, those sudden awarenesses that someone would die in the studio ended, and they have never occurred to me since.

Chapter 9

A Flow of Financial Blessings

G od has used telethons to keep Cornerstone TeleVision afloat financially.

Our early telethons lasted two weeks. Still, only occasionally would we make the goals (which were always absolute minimums). We resolved to shorten them anyhow—to 13 days, to 11, to 10, to 9, to 8 days. At eight days the telethons didn't reach the necessary goals, but we have persisted in trying to shorten them.

I've often said, "The Lord always asks us to do one more project than we can afford." That's what Wendell Wallace used to call "daring faith"—"walking always in victory, but ever on the edge of disaster." We have learned to walk relatively comfortably on the deep water, knowing from years of experience that God will keep us afloat.

Cornerstone TeleVision has enjoyed so many financial miracles through two decades that there is no question this is a God-breathed, supernatural ministry. The emotional swings between disaster and victory, however, can take their toll on us weak humans.

Norma, Russ, Father Mike Salvagna, celebrating a telethon victory with a guest.

Norma and Linda Shore dancing before the Lord.

A Flow of Financial Blessings

Amazingly, during all these years of financial testing, the gospel continues to be presented 24 hours every day. Christian television is like a "divine shotgun": many pellets miss their target, but some always hit their mark.

That is why we try to include programs for all ages and all types of people. And God seems pleased.

I have repeatedly been amazed at how God brings along the exact person we need to fill a specific position.

Always "fussy" about proper spelling and grammar, I am deeply embarrassed by misspelled words on the television screen, and I insist that we do our best to avoid such errors. In fact, part of the test we give potential secretaries is a 20-word spelling quiz.

After my first secretary resigned, we began interviewing applicants. When the results of the spelling quiz were tabulated, only one applicant received a perfect score. In fact, she is the *only* person ever to spell all 20 words correctly.

"That's the one I want!" I said.

So Ruth Coles, a lovely African-American woman, made a wonderful secretary for a number of years—until a large company made Ruth an offer she couldn't afford to turn down.

Near the end of 1980, Bill Freeman felt led to resign as general manager and return to CBN.

Oleen Eagle was available for the job, but I didn't feel that she was ready for it. After a year-and-a-half on the air, we were still struggling not only financially but also with a myriad of other problems.

I felt that we needed a man for the job—a *tough* man—and I told Oleen that. My problem was that I didn't realize how tough Oleen is.

When Oleen was nine years old, her mother died, leaving Oleen with the job of family cook. As a result, she grew up quite self-reliant and highly disciplined.

Oleen became a teacher of dressmaking, then went to work for Saks Fifth Avenue and later for Gimbel's Department Store in Pittsburgh. At Gimbel's, Oleen was the only woman on the store's 25-member management committee.

"How did you get along with all those men?" I asked her.

"Oh, it was easy. I just let them know I wouldn't go to bed with any of them, and we got along fine."

Oleen doesn't have a feminist chip on her shoulder as do some women executives. I appreciate that about her. Although she is very feminine and dresses tastefully (she makes many of her own outfits), Oleen actually considers herself "just one of the guys."

"I *know* God has called me to Cornerstone TeleVision!" she often says. And with that attitude, she goes about her business, trying to please not man, but God.

Occasionally Norma will share a word of wisdom with me at home, and I will come to work and hear the very same word confirmed by Oleen. At that point, I simply shake my head, marveling at the ways of God.

W hen Bill Freeman departed, Oleen realized it wasn't God's time for her yet. For the next six years, she continued to learn television.

A Flow of Financial Blessings

We hired David Kelton of the *PTL Club* as our new general manager. A skilled negotiator, David immediately began to dig us out of some serious problems.

David had learned negotiating the hard way—on the streets of Charlotte, North Carolina. For 15 years he had lived in a world of alcohol, drugs, and crime, while his mother, a woman of great faith, prayed for him earnestly.

In 1972, after David was saved and delivered from a host of demons, he didn't know what to do for a job. His brother Tim suggested that, since David was good at carpentry, he should go over to a new ministry located in Charlotte—called the *PTL Club*—and volunteer to build their counseling desks.

Not accustomed to functioning in normal society, David hesitantly walked into the counseling room. Many of the prayer phones were ringing, but there was only one person there—a man who had a phone at each ear.

He nodded to David to pick up a phone. David looked confused, and the man continued to motion with his head: Answer a phone!

Finally, David picked up a ringing phone and answered tentatively: "Hello?"

A woman's desperate voice cried, "I'm going to commit suicide!"

David looked pleadingly to the man on the phones, but he was busy trying to pray with two callers at once.

David did not know what to say. He only knew what Jesus had done for him several weeks before, so he told the suicide caller about his salvation experience. And she got saved! After that, wild horses couldn't have kept David away from the counseling phones! He fell in love with Christian television.

Russ, Oleen Eagle, and David Kelton.

David's wife Brinda would tell me from time to time, "You are supposed to write David's testimony."

"Great!" I replied, but David was too embarrassed to reveal his former life.

Finally, I sensed it was God's time, and David reluctantly agreed. The two of us drove to the North Carolina coast and spent a week working on the manuscript.

Repeatedly I asked David, "Give me some of the details of your former lifestyle."

Every time he protested, "I don't remember many of the things that happened. I was 'stoned' most of the time. All I know is what my family and friends have told me."

After we arrived back in Pittsburgh, I sat down to flesh out the story. While I was writing, I felt very nervous. As soon as I reached the point of David's salvation, the nervousness left.

A Flow of Financial Blessings

I asked David, "Were you real nervous before you were saved?"

"Oh, all the time. That's why I drank so much."

Interestingly, Jean Stewart, the volunteer who did the typesetting for the book, had the same experience of nervousness until she, too, reached the point where David was born again.

Called *Chosen to Live,* the book received some accolades from Christian reviewers. Unfortunately it is now out of print, but David's testimony led to the salvation of many people, especially those in prison.

A mother sent a copy of *Chosen to Live* to her wayward son, who was living in Texas. After reading the book, Jimmy became very angry.

"David Kelton is a liar!" he told his mother. "Those incredible stories could never have happened." Actually, Jimmy was under conviction by the Holy Spirit.

While visiting his mother in the Pittsburgh area, Jimmy came—with a pistol in his pocket—to the television station. The conviction of the Holy Spirit was so strong that he had to kill the man responsible—David Kelton.

"David is not here," the receptionist told Jimmy, but he was insistent.

Steve Totin, who is also rather streetwise, came to talk to the angry man.

"No, I've got to talk to David Kelton!"

"Well, he's off today."

"I don't care. Tell him I need to see him!"

The receptionist called David at home, describing the man.

"I need to pick up something at the station anyway," David said. "So I'll come in."

While waiting for David, Steve began to talk to Jimmy about his many problems, explaining how Jesus can take care of them all. The man argued with Steve, but he was beginning to soften.

Sensing danger, Steve continued to talk and pray with him.

By the time David arrived, Jimmy was more subdued, and he talked rationally to David. Then he pulled out the pistol— and handed it to David! "I came here to kill you!" he confessed.

Steve's eyes got big, but David was accustomed to guns. Before he got saved, David had carried two pistols. In fact, he still has a gun collection.

David took Jimmy's pistol and proceeded to lead him to Jesus! It was an unusual pistol, and David actually bought it for his personal collection from this newly saved Christian!

A very intelligent man with an uncanny, street-smart knack for sizing up people and situations, David was cool under fire. These abilities came in handy during his early days as our general manager.

After several years, David had almost gotten us on a smooth course. I told David, "When you came to Pittsburgh, there were two worms crawling out of the can every day. Now you've got it down to one worm a week!"

I n spite of David's expertise, the Western Pennsylvania Christian Broadcasting Company was still seriously undercapitalized. We could not catch up financially.

A Flow of Financial Blessings

Our accountant, Bill Hopper, lay awake one night until 2:00 a.m., talking and praying and crying with his wife. "There is no way this ministry can survive financially," he told her. "I've decided to resign." Then Bill dropped off in a fitful sleep.

At that very time I had a ministry engagement in South Carolina. I left Norma at her mother's house in Virginia, then drove to my services. Jim Bakker was having another of his interminable fund-raisers, so I had scraped together $400, which I planned to give to Jim on the way back through South Carolina.

After watching the live *PTL Club,* I walked up on the stage to give Jim Bakker the $400 check. Jim spotted me at a distance of about 50 feet, and suddenly came running across the stage. He threw his arms around me: "Russ! The Lord just told me to give you a hundred thousand dollars!"

I was speechless! Rather awkwardly I offered Jim the WPCB-TV check for $400, and he accepted it most graciously.

One hundred thousand dollars! Jim is a very "giving" person, but that great gift was so supernatural! As soon as Jim recognized me, the Lord spoke to him to give us that precise amount: $100,000. My knees were almost like water.

I took the $100,000 *PTL Club* check with me in the car, planning to surprise our Board of Directors who were to meet on my first day back in Pittsburgh. The Lord very clearly told me to hand it to our Finance Director, Bill Hopper, who had been struggling so unsuccessfully to pay the bills.

After his presentation of the gloomy financial report to the Board of Directors, I laid the check in front of Bill. When he realized what he was looking at, Bill's body began to shake. The grief of months of seemingly fruitless struggle came out in great sobs. The rest of us began to wipe our eyes and to praise the Lord with breaking voices.

That afternoon, I passed the $100,000 check around the staff prayer meeting. Everyone was thrilled, and the meeting rang with praises.

Bill Hopper tearfully began to tell us how he and his wife had decided at 2:00 a.m. the night before that he should resign: "I realized that I couldn't put it all together."

God, we discovered again, is the Lord of 11:59 p.m. That is God's minute. It's the "miracle minute"! Only faith can keep us walking with Jesus one minute before disaster. Somebody has named Him, "Jehovah Nick-o-time."

Bill was so blessed as he paid all the old bills. He reminded me of a little boy on Christmas morning. Every bill over 60 days old was paid!

Perhaps the greatest blessing was that every one of WPCB-TV's employees realized anew that God's hand is on this ministry. I, too, recognized mournfully that my former attitude of blaming our troubles on the economy or the cable systems had been blocking God's sovereign hand of blessing for a long time.

I like to keep our viewers informed about what is happening at the station. Many wonderful folks hardly watch any other channel, and they care about our financial condition. During *Getting Together,* I shared about the grace of God in Jim Bakker's gift. During the next two weeks, many people I met commented excitedly about the $100,000 we had received.

That one gift, however, did not mean instant prosperity. All the long overdue bills had been paid, but we still were not current.

Many partners apparently thought we had all the money we needed, so they stopped giving for a while. As a result, we started to slip back on our bills again—60 days, then 90 days, and some even further.

A Flow of Financial Blessings

Jerry Barnard of San Diego.

Nevertheless, we had learned the secret: God is our source! Now we knew that He would take care of our finances.

During one of our nearly disastrous telethons, Oleen received a phone call.

"Hi! I'm Jerry Barnard, from San Diego. I'm in the Pittsburgh area, and I'm available tonight. Could I be of any assistance?"

None of us knew Jerry except for one employee who had lived on the West Coast. He beamed and exclaimed, "Get him in front of the camera and turn him loose!" So we did.

That evening all heaven caved in. It was the best ministry we'd ever had during a telethon, and it was also the greatest evening in pledges. The Lord had come through again!

After David Kelton took the job of general manager, a number of Christians at the *PTL Club* began contacting him to ask if we would hire them. We accepted those we needed—about 20 very competent people.

David Kelton became known at PTL as "the Pittsburgh Pirate," and we were all called "the Pittsburgh Stealers." WPCB-TV was even referred to as "PTL North."

We soon learned, however, why all these "PTLers" were leaving. They brought with them tragic stories of unethical behavior. They felt a righteous God would not continue to bless the *PTL Club* in spite of all the good that Jim Bakker was doing.

The day finally came when we knew that we had to take the *PTL Club* off our station. It was a heart-wrenching decision.

Over a period of several years, the Lord had given me four painful words about Jim Bakker, who was a good friend.

First, one day Jim Bakker will do something to injure all of Christian television. Second, Jim Bakker is experimenting with homosexuality. Third, Jim Bakker will lose everything he has built in South Carolina. Fourth, the Christians who have invested in Heritage USA will lose it all.

Of course, all four prophecies have since been verified.

I was torn—loving Jim Bakker and appreciating God's anointing on him, yet deeply disturbed by the activities in which he was involved. In the summer of 1985, we finally took the *PTL Club* off our station.

To put things in proper perspective, I'll share just one additional miraculous story about Jim Bakker.

Several years before the Keltons left PTL for Pittsburgh, Brinda had a mammogram. When she returned for the verdict, the doctor told Brinda that the lump in her breast was cancerous.

A telethon is a busy place.

Praying over the prayer requests and salvation reports.

From left to right: Dr. Mitch Nickols, Russ, Norma, Oleen Eagle, Jim Fitzgerald.

Black Buffalo (Ray Wilson) and Ron Hembree with Norma and Russ at Tele Missions Conference.

The first three local pastors to produce programs or services on WPCB-TV.

From left to right: Dr. Michael Wenning of Pleasant Hills Community Presbyterian Church; Dr. Isaac Green of Central Baptist Church; Pastor Robert Owen of South Hills Assembly of God; with Bill Freeman (standing).

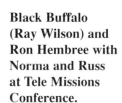

The TV 40 Singers, directed by Randy Estelle.

From left to right: Mike Hovanec, Ron Rice, Jan Kaufman, Marianne Mauti.

John Price and the Life Anew Singers of Madisonville, Kentucky.

Tom Green and friends on *Lightmusic*.

David Maloney and Tim Burgan "clown it up" at a telethon.

Richard Roberts and
Oleen Eagle during a telethon.

Reinhard Bonnke Crusade,
sponsored by Cornerstone
TeleVision at the
Pittsburgh Civic Arena;
24,000 people attended
two services.

Reinhard Bonnke Crusade
at Civic Arena.

Charles and Frances Hunter at the
groundbreaking for Stage One of
the "Isaiah 54 Project."

From left to right:
Norma, Russ, Roger
Wilson, Steve Totin,
Oleen Eagle.

In the foreground:
Verle Faust,
Brinda Kelton.

On the computers,
from left to right:
Tom Scott, Mary Pat
Leith, Patty Smith,
Kim Pierce.

Behind the cameras,
from left to right:
Carl McKown (behind),
Whitney Cicco,
Ray Heiple,
Ron Henderson.

Norma praying on the
phone during a telethon.

Ken Blose's heart was profoundly touched when he traveled to Mexico City to produce a TV segment for Chris Jones' ministry there. Ken returned home, promptly resigned from Cornerstone, and moved to Mexico to serve there. Through Ken's obedience, the Lord gave him a lovely wife, Juana.

Engineering Operations Supervisor Armand "Robbie" Roberts wearing his ever-present hat.

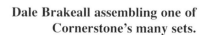

Eleanor Blazevich.

Dale Brakeall assembling one of Cornerstone's many sets.

Oleen Eagle at her desk.

Blake Richert and his wife Dee, who is Oleen Eagle's secretary.

Ronn Haus of TV 42, Concord, California, and Ben Armstrong of the National Religious Broadcasters presenting Cornerstone's "Station of the Year" award to Russ, Norma, and Oleen Eagle, 1985.

Norma's Super Seven prayer group.

From left to right: Lenore Boering, Nona Knerler, Maxine George, Eleanor Franz, Barbara Conner, Norma, Pauline Walton.

Cornerstone TeleVision's Board of Directors, January 1999. From left to right: Dr. Mitchel Nickols, Bill Roemer, Richard Simmons, Russ, Michelle Agatston, Oleen Eagle, Bill Pendleton, Gary Tustin, Dr. Bill Kofmehl.

Cornerstone TeleVision's "veterans," all of whom began to work no later than 1979. From left to right: Bob Taylor, Paul Bixler, Wes Kughen, Norma, Steve Totin, Paul McDonald, Russ, Josie Gutwerk, Oleen Eagle, David Skeba, Mary Anne Skeba, Gary Stewart.

The staff of Cornerstone TeleVision, daylight shift, 1998.

Russ and Norma's 50th anniversary celebration, January 1998, on the beach in Florida. Two more grandchildren have arrived since this photo was taken.

A Flow of Financial Blessings

She told the results only to David and David's mother, Myda Kelton, a remarkable woman of faith, and they prayed together. No one else knew.

That afternoon, after her doctor's appointment, Brinda immediately returned to work at the *PTL Club* because they were in the middle of a telethon, and Jim Bakker always liked to have Brinda Kelton on the adding machines.

That very afternoon Jim had a word of knowledge on the air: "God is healing someone of cancer of the breast! Call and tell us who you are."

"No-o-o...," Jim said slowly. "It's somebody in the studio audience! Who are you?"

Suddenly Jim wheeled around in his swivel chair, pointed at Brinda at her desk behind him, and exclaimed: "Brinda! It's you!"

Brinda went to the doctor as soon as she could, and the tumor was gone! That's the Holy Spirit anointing God has placed on Jim Bakker.

All of us at the station were heartbroken over the loss of PTL's ministry in the Pittsburgh area. At the same time, we could not continue to give our approval to actions that we knew were ungodly and unscriptural.

Many viewers, however, did not understand our decision. We received a lot of abuse on the phone and in the mail from those who disagreed with our position.

We continued to pray for Jim and Tammy Bakker throughout the trial and his imprisonment, and we rejoice at how God has since redeemed Jim Bakker and restored his life. Today it is becoming generally known that Jim was improperly convicted and imprisoned.

Chapter 10

Internal Struggle

One day David Kelton was laughing with me: "Russ," he said, "you know what they used to say about me at PTL? 'If everything is going smoothly, David Kelton will fix it.'"

I should have realized the significance of that statement, but I didn't. David is a natural "troubleshooter," but apparently he couldn't stand having everything peaceful.

His early years at the station were great, but he started trying to do too many things. We began falling behind in our finances.

"If you would give me the authority," David told me, "I could pull us out of this financial mess."

I decided to take a chance on David, but that decision was a mistake. Norma, with her discernment, opposed it, but Oleen and I went ahead anyway. As a result, after a number of faces changed on the Board of Directors, David pulled Norma and me off the air for several months in mid-1986.

I promptly said, "Lord, I didn't choose television; I'd much rather be ministering in the churches. I'll resign if You're finished with me here."

During those difficult months, Dr. Mitchel Nickols, a local pastor, stood solidly behind me, encouraging and counseling us. Mitch was an active member of our Ministry Advisory Board and later a long-time member of our Board of Directors. He is also an occasional guest host of *Getting Together.*

About this time Norma and I were speaking at a Women's Aglow banquet on a Saturday evening in northern Pennsylvania. That night Norma asked if we could visit Gospel Tabernacle, a famous church pastored by David Minor in tiny Coudersport, Pennsylvania. I checked the map and noted that if we left early in the morning, we could get there for the Sunday Worship Service.

We arrived at the church precisely at 11:00 a.m. Pastor Minor recognized me and invited me to the pulpit. Hardly anyone in the congregation knew us.

I had just been introduced when Tim Knapp, the pastor's son-in-law, jumped out from behind his drums and started shouting a prophecy! Tim knew nothing about me other than what Pastor Minor had said in his introduction.

These are the precise words of his prophecy, transcribed from the audiotape, with a few minor changes for grammatical purposes.

My son, the Lord has seen the desires of your heart, and that you have been as Moses, looking over Jordan, seeing the well-watered plants of the Promised Land. You have said in your heart, "I have seen it, but things have happened to me, and I shall not possess that which I have dreamed of."

Internal Struggle

My son, you shall lift your hands in the land I will give you, and you shall see an increase upon the right and the left. I will stir up finances, and you shall see people turn to you. Even many who have opposed you, whose names are upon your lips today, shall turn and say, "We shall stand with you and finance this thing," so that you shall see the purchase of much on My behalf, says the Lord, even a station that will send out My gospel over the airwaves.

My son, say not in your own heart, "I shall soon release this thing to another." You shall not, but you shall hold on to it ever the more tightly, and covet even that which is around about you—as you have said, "Yes, I have dreamed of it, but I shall not see it." For My son, I shall move on your behalf and you shall build and build....

Then Tim prophesied for Norma.

My daughter, the Lord would say to you, "You shall stir yourself in this hour and raise yourself upon your feet, taking the foundation that has been laid in you and speak to My people beside your husband. For, My daughter, I have called you to lead. I have called you to be a mighty warrior of faith and prayer.

"From time to time you shall rise up and shake yourself and take upon yourself the garment of a prophet and speak to women and men. Let them stand behind you— even as strength they will stand behind you. My daughter, I have called you to be a prophetess, that you should say, 'This is the way: walk in it!'

"Fear not; neither be timid nor draw back. Know that the Lord has called you to stand side by side with your husband in the ministry of the word of the Lord."

Well, we had our answer! We were breathless!

Only the Spirit of God could have given Tim Knapp those remarkable words. What incredibly accurate prophecies! Pastor Minor even took up an offering for Cornerstone.

Norma and I returned home to wait and pray.

Three additional, important events had already occurred.

First, we had the opportunity in early 1984 to purchase Channel 48, a station that was off the air in Philadelphia. We borrowed $700,000 from a local bank in Pittsburgh to purchase a television station worth far more than what we paid. However, we could not operate Channel 48 without the FCC's permission, and a lot of people contested us, filing their own applications.

Second, I had tried to talk to Jim Bakker, but he was by that time beyond listening; he apparently needed the therapy that the Lord was about to permit. Several years later, after Richard Dortch, Jim Bakker's Executive Vice President, was released from prison, Richard was a guest on *Getting Together*. He told our viewers that if all Christian stations had exercised Cornerstone's integrity, the Body of Christ might have been spared all that suffering.

A third event occurred when a pastor in Altoona, Pennsylvania, John Jameson, spoke to Norma and me at a meeting in that community: "Altoona's supposed to have a Christian television station, and you're to build it!"

I told David and Oleen about Pastor Jameson's word. David insisted that God said we were to build the station in Altoona,

156

but Norma and Oleen were opposed. I didn't have a leading either way.

Entrance to Channel 47's offices and studio in Altoona, Pennsylvania.

We could remove the Channel 48 transmitter from the darkened station in Philadelphia and modify it to Channel 47 for Altoona. That convinced me. We were then able to build the Altoona station at a very reasonable cost.

We only needed an additional $400,000. We created a "Four Hundred Club" for Christians who would invest $1,000 without interest.

Steve Totin's brother-in-law Freddie ridiculed the Four Hundred Club. "You'll never get 400 people to do that!"

Steve responded, "If you're so sure we won't make it, why don't you pledge number 400!"

"It's a deal," he responded. "If you get 399, I'll make it 400." And he laughed sarcastically.

The evening we reached 399, Steve Totin came on camera and challenged his brother-in-law—on air—and Freddie was watching. He phoned immediately and made good on his pledge.

Since then, whenever I meet Freddie, he always introduces himself with a grin, "Hi. I'm Agent 400."

So WKBS-TV, Channel 47, went on the air in central Pennsylvania, September 17, 1985.

Jack and Bobbi Foreman took the leadership in Altoona, assisting with the construction and the recruiting of prayer partners for the telephones. Without Jack and Bobbi, WKBS-TV wouldn't have made it. Later we invited Jack to join the Board of Directors.

The old roadhouse that we had purchased for a transmitter building had a crooked and broken concrete floor, as well as a leaky roof. Jack Foreman found two Christian contractors

Jack and Bobbi Foreman of Altoona, Pennsylvania.

whose businesses were in the doldrums, and they both agreed to do the repairs for the cost of the materials only.

Within days each contractor had new jobs rolling in. The Lord was showing them His appreciation. "But seek first his kingdom and his righteousness, and all these [material] things shall be yours as well" (Matthew 6:33).

Still, the daily operating expenses of the new station placed an additional, continuing strain on our finances. Today, however, WKBS-TV is sustaining itself financially quite well.

Pastor Rick Nicely, director of WKBS-TV.

While preparing to put WKBS-TV, Channel 47, on the air in central Pennsylvania, it became apparent that we needed another corporate name. The Western Pennsylvania Christian Broadcasting Company no longer described our growing ministry. After praying, considering, and rejecting some names, we settled upon Cornerstone Television, Inc.

I insisted, "Only if we capitalize the 'v' in television, because that's what it is—a Vision." So we became Cornerstone Tele-Vision, Inc.

During 1986 and into 1987, Cornestone's finances became desperate. Suddenly the bank announced that they were "calling the loan." This meant that, because we were delinquent in our payments, they wanted full payment of the remaining $500,000 we owed on the Philadelphia purchase—or they would foreclose on us.

At that very time, the PTL scandal broke around Jim Bakker's head. Everyone was confused about Christian ministries. Nearly all Christian organizations began to suffer losses, especially the television ministries. Even foreign missions suffered as a result of the scandal.

I talked privately to several of our Board members, and we agreed to release David Kelton, which we did in early April of 1987—just a couple of weeks after the PTL scandal broke. The future looked extremely bleak.

When the PTL mess was exposed in late March, we naively assumed that our viewers would commend us for having taken the *PTL Club* off the station a year-and-a-half earlier. It made no difference whatsoever. One-quarter of our donors simply quit! Instead of being pleased with our integrity, we were lumped together with Jim Bakker.

A Christian whom I know said, "Ah, they're all the same!" and stopped giving to Cornerstone TeleVision. I was shocked! And deeply hurt, too.

Even today I sometimes wonder if I have been fully healed of that bitter experience. Then I remember the three-fourths of our supporters who stayed with us, many of whom gave even more.

On April 15, Norma and I, along with Stan and Loretta Scott, told the viewers that we would have to go off the air unless God provided a financial miracle. "You have to decide. Do you really want a Christian television station?" We repeated that question over and over again: "You have to decide. Do you really want a Christian television station?"

Internal Struggle

Miraculously, for the next few days we were inundated with mail. The sudden rush of money paid off some old bills and kept us afloat for a few more weeks. We certainly knew most of the viewers were "partners" with us after that blessing.

"People really do care," we told one another.

In spite of this vote of confidence from our viewers, the bank loan still hung heavily over our heads. They wanted their $500,000.

The Lord told me that Oleen Eagle was to be our general manager, and that "she will enjoy the position." The Board agreed, and Oleen has done a fabulous job, enjoying nearly every moment. Today, of course, Oleen is president of Cornerstone TeleVision.

One of her first responsibilities was to ask the bank's vice president and lawyer if they would wait until June for their payment. They reluctantly agreed.

While we were in that deep trouble—the bank having called our loan, other creditors breathing down our necks, the PTL scandal fresh in everybody's mind, the daily financial drain by the Altoona station, Norma and Oleen both reminding me that we had run ahead of the Lord—God confirmed one day while I was mowing the lawn that, indeed, we had moved in Altoona ahead of the Holy Spirit.

"But Lord, You told us to build that station," I said.

"Whom did I tell?"

"Well, You told Pastor Jameson in Altoona...and You told David Kelton..." and, for the life of me, I could not recall His having told me.

"When I want to do something major at Cornerstone Tele-Vision," the Spirit concluded, "I'll tell *you*." And that was that!

This incident pointed out a problem that I've had for years—knowing in my spirit what should be done in a situation, but often deferring to others and to their wisdom. Most American Christians think that God's Kingdom should operate like America. My greatest fear was to be called a dictator, so I thought God should be "democratic," spreading the wisdom around in the Body of Christ.

I learned the hard way that God is "theocratic." The Bible reveals how God will frequently choose a single individual to speak for Him: No one else—just one. I know I've been chosen, but I'm often reluctant to assert my "chosenness."

With new boldness, I began to implement some changes that the Lord had been instructing me to make.

A t our Board meeting in early May I told the directors, "We need to begin tithing all our contributions. We're going down the tubes anyhow."

I then read to them the appropriate scripture from Numbers 18:26: "Moreover you shall say to the Levites, 'When you take from the people of Israel the tithe which I have given you from them for your inheritance, then you shall present an offering from it to the Lord, a tithe of the tithe.' "

"We've been grieving the Lord by not giving the tenth to other ministries," I added. "I feel certain that doing this will move the hand of the Lord on our behalf."

With a half-million-dollar debt to the bank staring us in the face, plus significant other indebtedness, God would have to move powerfully—and quickly. We swallowed hard and began giving away one-tenth of all our contributions.

We planned carefully and prayerfully how we would raise the half-million dollars for the bank.

"Pledges won't do," we all agreed. "We have to have cash—and quickly."

On June 12, 1987, we began fund-raising *live* every evening, five days a week, totaling the need and then showing our viewers each day's receipts. Since we didn't take pledges, we counted only the money that had been received that day. The Lord impressed on my heart that we should do it this way. Many Christians drove up our hill to deliver their gifts in person.

Each Monday we began to hold back up to $50,000 to take care of that week's operating needs for Cornerstone TeleVision. After we reached the $50,000 level, all the rest of the income that week went to the bank loan.

"At this rate, we could be raising funds for at least six months!" I told Oleen.

I sat down and prayed. Then I made a list of all our friends who had financial resources. Perhaps I could ask these friends for loans.

I looked over the list of about ten persons, and the Lord said, "None of them! Ask..."—and He then named two women, neither of whom was on my list. One was a widow who, I had heard, had been left impoverished by her husband. The other woman we hardly knew.

I felt very uncomfortable as I made the phone calls, but the Lord had clearly given me those two names.

First I called the widow. "We need to borrow $150,000," I told her.

Faith Works

She agreed to provide collateral for a bank loan of $45,000. I had been mistaken about her husband's estate; it was quite adequate.

Then I phoned the other woman, and she promptly agreed to loan us the remaining $105,000! I had no idea that either woman had that kind of money available.

About the end of June, the bank's lawyer and the vice president made an appointment to come to the station. They admitted later that they were planning to say, "Well, this isn't working. What do you propose now?"

We handed two astonished bankers a check for $150,000, and then added, "You'll be getting another $100,000 on Friday."

They were flabbergasted!

Soon I received a call from the lady who had loaned us the $105,000. "The Lord told me to make that loan a gift!" she stated.

Within six weeks—from early June into July—the entire $500,000 was paid! God had done it again, and our partners—the viewers—were the heroes!

The year of the PTL scandal, 1987, could have destroyed us—as it nearly did many other ministries—but God spectacularly rescued us.

Even after the bank had been repaid, the remaining debt we owed was still enough to bankrupt us. We continued to pray and trust God to provide.

In October we received the largest gift ever—$200,000—from another anonymous donor! That precious donor's gift saved this ministry!

Our accountant quickly paid Cornerstone's bills, and we ended that year—for the first time ever—current on all our bills!

Internal Struggle

Although many ministries experienced a severe drop in donations, our income was 22 percent above the previous year. It was the best year financially we'd ever had!

To God be the glory! The year 1987 was a watershed year for this ministry. The Lord brought victory out of what appeared to be certain disaster—and then started Cornerstone TeleVision growing again.

Chapter 11

God Enlarges the Vision

As long ago as February 1981, three days after David Kelton started his job as general manager, God proclaimed a new direction for Cornerstone TeleVision.

Oleen and I had walked into David's office, and I was standing as the three of us were talking. David drifted off the subject and said, "You know, Russ, I was thinking a couple of days ago—this ministry is supposed to be a *regional* ministry."

Instantly the Holy Spirit did those "cartwheels" in my spirit— exactly as He had done in 1969, when I fell over on the bed. This time I stumbled backward onto David's credenza, which was sitting in the middle of the room.

"David!" I shouted. "God just verified what you said!"

I then told Oleen and David what had happened more than 11 years earlier when John Zerby had proposed that we put out a fleece concerning my initial involvement in Christian television.

How could we become a regional ministry? I thought. In 1981, we were so deeply in debt from just one station that I couldn't

167

see beyond it. Yet there was that shocking word—and its equally shocking confirmation by the Spirit of God.

Within the next two years, I received a note from Dick Mills in California. He gave me a prophetic scripture, which he said the Lord had spoken for our ministry. It was Isaiah 54:2-3:

Enlarge the place of your tent, and let the curtains of your habitations be stretched out; hold not back, lengthen your cords and strengthen your stakes. For you will spread abroad to the right and to the left....

Within another year some of our guests on *Getting Together* began prophesying the same scripture: Tim Kelton, Mary Ann Brown, and several others. I am reminded of one line in Tim Knapp's remarkable prophecy at the church in Coudersport: "You shall see an increase upon the right and the left."

Soon we printed small signs of Isaiah 54:2-3 and placed them around the building as reminders of what God was going to do for us. And the Lord has long since more than fulfilled His promise! What God says, He does!

It seems the more prayer we receive, the better everything works. That should be obvious to all of us, but we don't always live as if we know it.

Cornerstone TeleVision now has a small army of organized prayer warriors to whom we mail lists of priority items for prayer. One of our part-time employees has the sole responsibility of coordinating the intercessory prayer ministry and supplying intercessors with lists of prayer projects.

In addition to mandatory prayer and Bible study meetings, some of Cornerstone's staff meet voluntarily during their lunch hour each day to intercede for this ministry.

God Enlarges the Vision

About this same time, I learned the importance of persistent intercessory prayer in a very personal way.

Years ago my dad and mother came to hear me when I was preaching in a church about 12 miles from their home in Westminster, Maryland. They had been attending a Baptist Church for several years, but they weren't born again.

When I invited people to come forward to be baptized in the Holy Spirit, Dad and Mother shocked me by coming up the aisle with all the other folks. I was astonished. They had heard me preach a number of times before, but I had seen no response in them.

Dad had always refused to read the Bible. "I can't understand that black Bible!" he would exclaim, meaning, of course, the King James Version. So Norma had suggested that we give him The Living Bible for his 80th birthday.

The next time we visited, Dad was excited. "I can understand this Bible—for the first time in my life!"

We learned that Mother had been sneaking opportunities to read his Bible, too. Now, exactly six months later, the Bible reading had obviously opened their hearts.

Seeing Dad and Mother walk the aisle of that church was a very emotional moment for me. I carefully and thoroughly explained God's plan of salvation, and then led everyone in a salvation prayer.

Constantly on the verge of tears, I followed by praying with everyone to receive the Holy Spirit.

My parents were absolutely transformed! I know! I grew up in that home! At the time, Dad was 80 and Mother 69. Dad's final 14 years were the happiest of his life.

In late January 1987, during the telethon time, I learned that Dad was about to "graduate" at the grand age of 94. My parents were then living in Florida, at Christian Retreat, and I knew my presence was not necessary there.

When I received the message that Dad was dying, our producer asked, "Would you like to stay off the air this evening?"

"Oh, no!" I protested. "Now I've *got* to be on the telethon!"

Instead of fund-raising, I shared my Dad's wonderful testimony, crying a good deal while I was talking and inviting unsaved viewers to call and accept Jesus as Lord.

The next afternoon Dad graduated, and everyone was sure I'd take off for the evening. But the Lord spoke to me: "Life must go on!" I knew exactly what He meant.

We Christians need the power of the Holy Spirit to live victoriously and to enable us to fulfill the Great Commission. That evening I urged folks to get baptized in the Holy Spirit, as Dad had been.

In my father's "homecoming," he led more people to the Lord than ever before. Ninety-five persons accepted Jesus on the phones during those two evenings, and 104 were baptized in the Holy Spirit. Dad would have loved it!

That was one of the happiest funerals we ever attended—my own dad's.

We began to believe God to provide additional ministry programs. Actually, we had started some other programs earlier, but with limited success. David Kelton taught us the vital lesson that good, locally-produced programs are the keys to successful Christian television.

God Enlarges the Vision

Ron Hembree, a great preacher and teacher, came to work for Western Pennsylvania Christian Broadcasting Company in 1983. Ron developed a successful program called *Rejoice!* on which he ministered until he was called to be the senior pastor of First Assembly of God in Rockford, Illinois, in 1984.

We developed a special relationship with Ron during that period—a relationship that would become very important later. Before he left to pastor the huge congregation in Rockford, I asked Ron, "Who is preaching at the church in the interim since the former pastor has already gone?"

Ron answered, "It's no problem. They still have 23 pastors on the staff!"

For years, I had been troubled about how most Christians— pastors included—simply do not perceive the destruction caused by the theory of evolution. Few realize that evolution forms the philosophical/scientific basis for socialism, communism, naziism, racism, euthanasia, abortion, atheism, occultism, New Age religion, various other religions, high crime rates, declining educational standards, the steady deterioration of constitutional law—yes, all those, and more.

The theory of evolution goes beyond theory and falls into the realm of *impossibility!* It violates the First and Second Laws of Thermodynamics, as well as the Laws of Biogenesis and of Cause and Effect. Few people know that fact; scientists rarely admit it. Most scientists who know the absurdity of evolution don't dare mention it publicly. Why? They are afraid of their peers.

The logical question of the sixteenth-century Protestant reformer John Calvin still remains unanswered by evolutionists after nearly 500 years: "How could the creation possibly create itself?" Calvin's question demonstrates how easily the human mind can deceive itself.

Why do many educated people hold so emotionally to the false theory of evolution? Because, if creation is true, then they owe their allegiance to the Creator, and sinful human nature is absolutely opposed to commitment to God.

Further, evolutionists won't admit to the worldwide reality of Noah's flood. Why not? For scientific reasons? No. But because the universal flood speaks of God's judgment upon sin.

Christians are often so gullible that they invent or accept implausible theories of creation—like the gap theory, progressive creation, the literary framework theory, or theistic evolution—all of which violate the Book of Genesis as well as the scientific testimony. Many Christians have been compromising on these issues because they tend to believe the so-called "experts."

In 1985, I felt God's leading as we developed *Origins,* a teaching program dealing with creation issues from both biblical and scientific perspectives. Now carried on many stations across the nation, it is the only program of its kind. One other similar program airs on a different Christian network, but it does not hold to the biblical testimony of the six-day creation or to the worldwide flood. *Origins* remains the only television program that explains the myths of evolution and presents the facts of the Genesis creation and Noah's flood.

Evolutionists are not accustomed to being opposed in the public arena. The news media, being largely ignorant of the scientific data, continually misrepresent creationism. Whenever a debate is held, if the creationist knows his science, the evolutionist almost always loses the debate.

Aircraft designer Luther Sunderland on *Origins, with Russ*.

Why do our young people often reject Christianity? Because the teaching of evolution in public schools blinds them to the truth. Evolutionist educators are terrified whenever the evidence *against* evolution is presented in our schools. *Origins* serves two objectives: To strengthen the faith of Christians and to confound evolutionists.

One of the greatest curses in the American Church is what we call liberalism, which is little more than the theory of evolution *forced upon* the Bible. Liberalism in the Church is merely a symptom of the deeper, causative sickness—the theory of evolution. Whenever a "liberal" pastor discovers for himself the fact that this theory is quite *unscientific*, that pastor will almost always move toward accepting the inerrancy of the Bible.

I was thrilled about a phone call one day from a chemistry professor who teaches at an eastern college.

He told us, "I used to delight in poking fun at my creationist students until one student videotaped an *Origins* program and challenged me to watch it."

That particular segment featured a discussion of Neanderthal Man, taught by one of the world's foremost authorities on that subject. As the chemistry professor listened to the indisputable facts being presented, he suddenly realized that the evolutionist "experts" on Neanderthals had been deliberately lying about the evidence. He became an instant creationist! And he is being mentored by the guest expert from that *Origins* program.

I n 1983, Arlene Williams came to work for Cornerstone TeleVision, where she helped in our Partner Services Department. Arlene did several other jobs adequately, so we asked, "Would you like to produce *Getting Together*?"

"Oh, I don't know," Arlene replied hesitantly. "I don't have any experience in television."

We gave her the job anyway. She learned quickly and did quite well for several years.

One day God spoke to my heart, "Arlene should have a cooking program."

I asked Norma, "Do you sense anything in your spirit about this?"

"Yes," she agreed.

So we asked Arlene to come to our office where I shared this word of the Lord with her. Arlene was not fazed at all.

Arlene Williams, host of *At Home*.

"Now I'll tell *you* something," she responded. "Last Christmas, we had scheduled a guest for *Getting Together* to do some holiday cooking as part of the program. When she canceled, I decided to do it myself.

"The next Sunday morning," Arlene continued, "a member of our church told me that his brother-in-law, an advertising executive in New York, had been visiting them and had seen me cooking on *Getting Together*."

Arlene then told us that, after watching the program, this advertising executive had said, "You tell that woman that if she will come to New York, I'll put her on TV with her own cooking show, and within a year it'll be national!"

This advertising executive recognized that Arlene has natural talent for television.

"I only told a few people about this conversation, including Oleen," Arlene explained to Norma and me. "So I just prayed: 'Lord, if this is of You, You'll have to bring it to pass.' " Then she smiled at Norma and me.

"And you were just like Mary," I responded happily, "pondering these things in your heart. No one had ever mentioned anything to me about your doing a cooking show until the Lord brought it up!"

We immediately began making preparations for *At Home With Arlene Williams.* A lot of planning and work were involved—especially in building the kitchen set—but the new cooking program went on the air in 1991. It ran for five years until Arlene told us that she felt God leading her to do a syndicated program for secular television.

At Home turned out to be an extremely popular program.

I am not a "joiner." Whenever I am asked to join the board of directors of a charitable organization, I usually refuse, suggesting someone else.

For some reason, however, I have always sensed the importance of belonging to the Board of the National Religious Broadcasters. Elected to the Board of Directors in 1984, I have been reelected continuously ever since.

The majority of "fundamentalists" at the NRB didn't quite trust us charismatics. Slowly, however, they discovered that we don't bite, and we have worked together quite well ever since. Some of our most important contacts have been made at the annual NRB Conventions.

Russ speaking at the National Religious Broadcasters Convention.

In addition, membership in the NRB is conditional upon joining the Evangelical Council for Financial Accountability. The ECFA is a rather strict organization that enforces honesty and integrity in handling finances, and Cornerstone TeleVision is proud to be a member.

The heart of the prayer partner.
(Drawing by Waltraud Hendel.)

Chapter 12

Prayer Partners—The Heart of the Ministry

O ne of Cornerstone TeleVision's core services has been the telephone prayer lines. Volunteers man the phones when we present *Getting Together.* At other times we use diverters to direct the prayer calls to the homes of volunteers, and we try to have somebody available around the clock.

One evening I was relaxing on the *Getting Together* set during a song, and my eyes were scanning the prayer partners. I noticed one of the women sitting quietly with the phone at her ear, listening to the caller. Down each cheek rolled a tear as she was obviously listening to a tragic story. That picture exemplifies for me the heart of our prayer partners.

One day David and Brinda Kelton walked into a business office in Pittsburgh, where the receptionist recognized them. She burst into tears of joy: "My husband walked out on me when I was eight months pregnant. I almost went crazy! I called your prayer line every day, sometimes twice a day. But God answered all those prayers! My daughter and I are together; I have this nice job, and we're happy. Praise the Lord! And—thank you for being there when I needed you!"

Thousands of such thrilling stories could be told; they occur nearly every day. Most of the miracles happen on the telephones, including an astonishing number of averted suicides. The pain and suffering in this world are almost unbelievable. Our prayer partners have heard it all, and they share lovingly in the callers' distresses.

In our early days, Dee Capets received a call from a lady who said that she was blind. Dee told her to place her hand over her eyes during the prayer. This woman called back 15 minutes later to report that she could see!

I wish we had followed up on this reported miracle, but we cannot verify it; Dee only knew what the lady told her on the phone.

Whenever callers accept the Lord on the prayer phones, we make an effort to follow up and ask how they are doing and if they are reading the Bible and the materials we sent them. We also urge them to "find a good church." We at Cornerstone realize that we are not called to be their local church.

The apostle Paul gives us a scripture that fits Christian television in a remarkable way.

> *Then Isaiah is so bold as to say, "I have been found by those who did not seek Me; I have shown Myself to those who did not ask for Me"* (Romans 10:20).

We have found this verse to be true at Cornerstone.

People casually "grazing" across the dial with their remotes will see something on Cornerstone TeleVision that catches their eye—and presto! The Spirit of God hooks them with the gospel. It happens every day!

180

Prayer Partners—The Heart of the Ministry

One evening, a 19-year-old girl was calling a friend but dialed the wrong number. It turned out to be the "right" number. As the prayer partner continued talking to her, she committed her life to Jesus Christ.

Another time, a man phoned our prayer number, asking, "Is this QVC?" He obviously wanted to order one of QVC's products.

The prayer partner kept telling him, "No, you did dial the right number." He, too, ended up being born again.

Indeed, God is quite often found by those who aren't looking for Him.

I asked a few of our long-time prayer partners to recall their favorite miracles. I hope the reader is as blessed as I was when these partners shared their own special memories.

As soon as TV 40 came on the air, Beverly Aurednik began calling night after night for prayer for her husband's salvation. After many dozens of calls and nearly one year later, he accepted the Lord and, within two weeks, all their children also came to Jesus. Beverly was so grateful that she became a prayer partner herself and is still faithful after nearly 20 years.

Faye Baldwin, a registered nurse, took a call from a lady who was hemorrhaging severely from a fibroid tumor. Blood was flowing into her bladder and down her leg, but she refused to go to the hospital.

"Everything in my nurse's training wanted to scream, 'Call an ambulance!'" Faye remembers. "But I knew I should pray immediately for the bleeding to stop. So I asked the Lord to melt the tumor and cauterize the leaking blood vessels.

"When I returned to the prayer phones the following week, Steve Totin told me that this woman wanted to talk to me. When I called her, the lady said, 'When you prayed, I felt intense heat around my uterus. The pain and the bleeding both stopped at that moment.'

"Later she called again to tell that she went to her doctor for a sonogram; it came back negative. The doctor told her a tumor that size never disappears, so he ordered another sonogram. It came back negative also!"

I think it's remarkable how the Spirit of God directs phone calls to the right person: an alcoholic to a former alcoholic, a cancer sufferer to a cancer victor, and so on.

George and Pauline Walton have been very special friends since 1970. They used to attend the Sunday evening services at the Pittsburgh Church of the Brethren. George had been suffering with a skin disorder on his hands when he first began coming to our church.

Don Scarborough praying with a caller.

"One Sunday evening there was a word of knowledge perfectly describing my condition," said George. "I looked down at my hands, and dead skin was falling on the floor. Shocked, I realized God was healing me. I've never had the problem since that evening."

During a telethon (when an unusual number of miracles tend to occur), a lady phoned about a skin disorder on her

182

son's legs. And, very appropriately, the Spirit of God directed the call to George Walton.

"I told her how God had healed me years ago of the same condition," said George. " 'Put your son on the telephone,' I instructed her.

"I started to pray in tongues first, but the Spirit of God stopped me: 'Tell him to look at his legs.' Suddenly the boy started screaming! Dead skin was falling on the floor, and new skin was forming in its place. Within moments he was totally healed just as I had been many years ago!"

One evening Steve Totin told the prayer partners to try to keep the calls short: "We don't have enough prayer partners," he explained.

Lorraine Cinciripini's first call came from a hysterical young girl who was scheduled to have an abortion the next morning. "In spite of Steve's instructions," Lorraine told us, "I had to stay on the phone the full hour. Finally I said, 'Give me your number and I'll call you back from home.' And I spent another three hours with her.

"The girl was under intense pressure from others to abort her baby. The next evening the girl phoned again—when I was answering the diverter phone in my home—to tell me that she did not have the abortion, and during that call she committed her life to Jesus.

"But the story doesn't end there. Many months later the young lady phoned to tell me that she was now married and had another baby. Then she told me that her girlfriend had been scheduled for an abortion, and she had told the girlfriend everything the Holy Spirit had given me to tell her several years before. And her friend also decided not to have an abortion; she had twins."

Three babies saved through that one very personal ministry!

Lorraine continued, "Recently she called me again. Her little boy had been severely scalded by boiling water, and we prayed together. 'The doctor was amazed,' she told me later. 'There are no scars at all from those burns!' "

One important truth may be learned from Lorraine's story. Burns respond remarkably to prayer! Whenever someone is burned severely, call for prayer *first*, and then go to the hospital. *Continuing* prayer for burn victims is essential also. Everyone concerned will be amazed at what God does. We witnessed how God had hastened the healing process for Jimmy Quinn's burns after the explosion in 1978.

M el Wenger, who had been a prayer partner from the day we went on the air, prayed with a lady who said her husband had left her for another woman. This tragedy led her to accept Jesus as Lord.

Eager prayer partners waiting for calls.

Prayer Partners—The Heart of the Ministry

Later, as Mel would occasionally answer this woman's repeated phone calls, she said the Lord had told her He would bring her husband back. After perhaps hundreds of prayers by our prayer partners, this caller's husband returned to her in 1995 —following *nine years of prayer!* They were remarried, and this miracle has caused many to realize the efficacy of continuing prayer (see Luke 11:5-13; 18:1-8).

Nora Holmes also prayed often for this same lady. Nora suggested that she read her scriptural promises out loud: "A word has no power until it is spoken," added Nora.

The caller began this oral reading of scriptural promises with her Christian neighbor. Along the way, other blessings occurred to both of them. In addition, the *neighbor's* wandering husband also came home after six years away—and got saved!

Augie Jordan shared a couple of his stories.

"A drunk phoned, and I told him I understood; before I became a Christian I had been a heavy drinker, too.

"This man confessed that he had once been a Christian—in fact, a pastor. His wife had left him and, as a result, he began to drink, and it cost him his pastorate. He had been filled with resentment and bitterness ever since. Now he was wondering if God still loved him.

"I prayed with him for deliverance from alcohol, led him through a prayer of rededication, and then the Lord baptized him in the Holy Spirit. Suddenly this despondent former pastor was rejoicing in his acceptance by the Lord!"

185

Augie also remembers this dramatic miracle: "A mother called during a telethon for prayer for her son who had been in a mental institution for some time. I prayed with her for deliverance for her son's mind.

"The next evening she called back and, remarkably, the Spirit of God directed her call to me again. She said her son had just phoned and told her that something had happened the evening before: His mind had suddenly cleared! He spoke to the doctors, and they agreed that there was no need for him to stay. They released him from the hospital, and he was coming home."

A man phoned Priscilla Gulasky, a prayer partner since 1980, to say that he was going to commit suicide. "I've been going to church, and I've been praying, but my prayers never get answered. Nothing ever goes right. I don't think there's a God out there, so I'm going to end it all."

Priscilla told him over and over that Jesus loved him and had a plan for his life. "I asked him to copy some helpful scriptures, which he did. He then rededicated his life to the Lord, and I told him to find a good church.

"Later, he called again when I was on the prayer phones and thanked me for the scriptures, saying that they had indeed been helpful. As we talked, he told me where he lived, and I realized that he lived near my church, so I suggested he go there."

One Sunday morning Priscilla was at her church when the pastor's wife told her, "There's a man here who wants to see you." It was the very man who had been planning suicide. He began attending services there, and today he is the drummer for the congregation's worship team!

186

Prayer Partners—The Heart of the Ministry

Steve Totin took a call from a distraught mother, whose son Ralph was to have his leg amputated the next morning. "He's so young, and the bone cancer is spreading. I just can't believe this is happening to my son."

Steve asked, "Do you believe in miracles?"

"Well, I've been praying a lot for Ralph, but the doctors say the leg has to come off."

"But do you believe in miracles?"

"Yes."

"Can you believe for a miracle for your own son?"

"That's so close to home. I don't know if I can believe for that miracle."

"I'm going to take authority over that bone cancer in the name of Jesus, the name above every other name."

She repeated that she didn't know if she could believe.

Steve continued, "I'm going to pray now, and if you can agree with me, say 'Yes, Lord.'" And Steve prayed.

"You pray different from other people," she commented.

"Well, we have authority over cancer, and we have to exercise that authority. Now, in the morning you ask the doctors to take another X-ray before they amputate Ralph's leg."

"Oh, I couldn't do that! They just checked today. That's what caused them to make the decision to amputate."

"No, no. You need to tell them to X-ray his leg again. You're his mother, and you have that privilege!"

She said she would.

The doctor argued with her the next morning. "We must amputate immediately to save your son's life!" But the mother insisted on one more X-ray.

The mother called Steve, rejoicing. "All the cancer is gone!" she shouted. "I've never before believed that much in miracles. When the doctor started talking to me about fitting Ralph with an artificial limb, I began seeing that prosthesis in my mind. Now I believe that Jesus has the power to heal cancer!"

After we went on satellite, one of our first affiliate stations was a low-power channel in Salem, Oregon. Several weeks later we were having a telethon, and a young woman phoned all the way from Oregon to make a ten-dollar pledge: "It's all I can afford now."

The prayer partner thanked her and asked if he could pray for her. "Well, my husband walked out on me and our three children six months ago. Please pray that God will send him back home."

He prayed a very anointed prayer.

Within two or three hours this wayward husband called his wife, asking if he could come over and discuss his coming home. The ecstatic wife phoned right back—from Oregon—and made another ten-dollar pledge. After her husband returned, she called back with a *third* pledge.

We are accustomed to hearing of *financial* blessings from seed sowing, but we are especially thrilled to hear how the Lord has done other types of miracles in response to faith pledges.

Prayer Partners—The Heart of the Ministry

Prayer partners busily praying for needy callers.

Martha Baker, who has probably served more hours on the prayer phones than anyone else, tells her favorite story.

A young woman who was separated from her husband called and accepted Jesus as Lord. While this miracle was occurring and the prayer partner was still praying for the marriage to be restored, a second phone rang and was answered by another prayer partner. It was the first caller's estranged husband, phoning to accept Jesus also!

When one of our staff was going over the prayer requests and salvation reports, they realized that this was the very man who had been prayed for by the other prayer partner.

God had used Christian television simultaneously to reach an estranged husband and wife living at different locations. Two special miracles of salvation and restoration occurred. A very different husband returned home to a very different wife.

Faith Works

Patricia was born into an abusive family. By the age of two she was already developing a multiple personality disorder. All through her childhood she suffered from abusive men, and she found escape by dissociation.

Through the years Pat actually picked up a total of about 100 different "personalities." These personalities actually provided entertainment for Pat's friends and family: The personalities would carry on conversations as they were called by name.

Pat suffered with this multiple personality disorder for 40 years; the condition had become so severe that she was placed on disability in her early 30's. Complicating the problem was her involvement in occultism, such as the Ouija board and tarot cards.

One day Pat discovered Cornerstone TeleVision, and she was literally consumed with the message of the gospel. She began watching day and night, taking breaks only to cook and clean her house.

Pat says, "I ate, drank, and slept Cornerstone TeleVision for a year. I called the prayer partners occasionally, repenting of anything that seemed to be sin."

The greatest miracle occurred when Pat committed her life to Jesus Christ with a Cornerstone prayer partner.

In November 1995 she was watching Cornerstone TeleVision while Richard Roberts was sharing. Richard was recounting his testimony of inheriting a 42-million-dollar indebtedness when he was named president of Oral Roberts University, and how he began to laugh, followed by miracles of financial deliverance.

While Richard was laughing on television, Pat began to laugh also. She laughed all day—for four days! "But," she

190

added, "it wasn't a laugh like when there is something funny. It was genuinely of the Holy Spirit."

Four days later Pat realized to her delight that all those personalities were gone. "It took four days of laughing to notice that I was different; there was no inner dialogue anymore. I tried calling one of these personalities by name, and nobody was there!" And Pat just laughed some more.

Slowly Pat's family and friends began to realize that she was a new person, and this miracle has made a great impact on the lives of many others.

"Before, when I had a problem, I would just dissociate. Now, whenever there's a problem, I call the prayer line and give it to God."

Within weeks Pat began ministering at a rescue mission; she plays the guitar and sings praises to the Lord.

A psychologist friend invited Pat to speak to a convention, and there she was allowed to give her testimony of how Jesus Christ had made her whole. "I suffered with this for 40 years, but it took God only four days to fix it!"

M ike was contacted by one of our associates, asking if he would be willing to contribute to Cornerstone TeleVision the same amount he had given the previous year. He stated that he couldn't contribute because some of his funds had been tied up.

Later, as he was watching the telethon, Mike knew he should pledge in spite of the fact that his money was not available. So he phoned and pledged—not the amount he had given the year before, but double! The next day Mike received a call that his funds were going to be released that very month.

From Homestead, Pennsylvania, came this miracle report: "Thank you for your prayers for my son. God has set him free from homosexuality."

Shirley called the prayer line because of carpal tunnel syndrome in both hands. She later sent us this note: "I want to thank the Lord for healing both of my hands of carpal tunnel syndrome through Channel 40. Praise God!"

And another testimony: "Brother Steve prayed for my niece, and she was healed of cancer. She is still clean after three years."

Delores reported that she had phoned for prayer for her uncle who was suffering from both brain cancer and lung cancer. "It was during a *Getting Together* program while the guest, Ken Gaub, was praying specifically for cancer," she told us.

The very next day Delores' 75-year-old uncle phoned her. He was crying, claiming that he had been healed by the Lord Jesus Christ. He said he saw a bright light flash in his head, and a warm glow went through his entire body. That very day the uncle accepted Jesus as his Lord and daily continued to get stronger in his body.

Occasionally the Lord reveals His sense of humor on television.

One evening the Lord gave me this word: "There's a man watching who is so desperate about finances that he feels as if he has a brick in the pit of his stomach. The Lord says He is going to provide the money you need."

Prayer Partners—The Heart of the Ministry

Almost immediately a viewer phoned to say I had described him perfectly. "A warm feeling went over my entire body, and the 'brick' disappeared promptly," he told the prayer partner.

The next day this man bought a winning lottery ticket, then in his joy sent our ministry ten percent of his jackpot! I realize that God does not approve of such gambling; I only report what He did for one man. I think it reveals the Lord's sense of humor as well as His creativity.

Charlotte Burgan and Bob Redinger praying. Peg Heaps and Martha Baker (in background) waiting for calls.

Millie took her husband home from the hospital in spite of the doctor's strong protests. Sonny was so severely crippled with multiple sclerosis that he was in a fetal position, unable to walk or talk, and totally out of control.

Millie would lie beside her husband at home, singing praises and praying for him. She began calling Cornerstone TeleVision for prayer for Sonny, and he gradually started to walk and talk again. At one point, when Millie called for prayer, she was crying because her husband wasn't eating, and she was panic-stricken.

"The voice on the phone was so sweet," she said, "like an angel's. I began to cry as a feeling like a blanket came over me, like a covering of peace. His voice was so sweet, but so strong; it was as if I had a connection to heaven. The joy and peace were indescribable."

After five years of Millie's love and care at home, Sonny went to be with the Lord. It had been five years of difficulties, yet there were repeated times of glorious miracles and deliverance.

Today Millie does hospital visitation, wandering from room to room and praying for anyone she can.

"Cornerstone is one of the greatest things God has given us," she adds. "Russ and Norma are real; there is nothing false about them. They were there for us; they encouraged us to visit the healing services. Norma came and hugged us, making us feel so welcome. Russ even pushed my husband up to the front in his wheelchair. They are tried and true."

Shannon Gould of Somerset, Pennsylvania, with her foster sister, performing on *Getting Together*, while Father Mike Salvagna and Ernie Frederick watch.

Prayer Partners—The Heart of the Ministry

Many hundreds have been healed right in our studio, especially during the miracle services. One very touching healing occurred following a normal *Getting Together,* in which two little foster children had performed ballet for the viewers.

One of the girls, Shannon, was eight years old and had come from a horribly dysfunctional home life. When she joined the Gould family of Somerset, Pennsylvania, she ate her food with her fingers.

As the family was preparing to leave the studio that evening, we learned that Shannon was suffering from cystic fibrosis.

"If you could wait for a few minutes," I told them, "I'd like to share about a little boy in Virginia who was instantly healed of cystic fibrosis when Norma had a word of knowledge in the boy's church."

After I told the story, I prayed for Shannon.

Later Shannon's foster mother shared that all the symptoms of cystic fibrosis promptly disappeared. Shannon's healing miracle that evening was just one of numerous evidences of God's grace in her young life.

A woman in suburban Pittsburgh was terribly despondent. She had undergone serious cancer surgery and was on chemotherapy. Her husband had divorced her, and her daughter had just moved out, leaving the mother alone. Only suicide could solve her problems.

She had attached a belt overhead, climbed up on a chair, and buckled the belt around her neck. Her television set was tuned to Cornerstone TeleVision, and, as she was getting up the courage to jump, she heard Norma and me introduce *Getting Together.*

Norma said something I don't recall her ever saying before: She suggested that people contemplating *suicide* should call for prayer, "...if you're at the end of your rope."

"That's right!" I exclaimed forcefully. "Call for prayer if you're at the end of your rope!"

Norma continued, "As someone has said, 'When you're at the end of your rope, tie a knot and hang on to Jesus.' "

This lady suddenly realized that Jesus knew her address and had singled her out. She carefully undid the belt, got off the chair, and phoned our prayer line.

Marge Miller answered the call and spent nearly the entire program talking and praying. The woman had once been a Christian but had walked away from Jesus. Marge led her in a prayer of rededication, then prayed that she be filled with the Holy Spirit. The woman began praying in tongues, and soon she was overflowing with the joy of the Lord—in spite of her outward circumstances.

All of us were in tears as we gave the good news in the final minute of the program, and Norma exclaimed, "Cornerstone TeleVision is indeed 'life-changing television'!"

Nine days later this grateful woman phoned in a telethon pledge of $1,000! God had used Cornerstone TeleVision to save her life.

In addition to the requests called in by phone, thousands of personal prayer needs are sent to Cornerstone TeleVision through the mail. Normally, these accompany contributions to the ministry. We take those prayer needs seriously and try to pray at least once for every request.

Prayer Partners—The Heart of the Ministry

R ichard Roberts, President of Oral Roberts University, has a very special, God-given anointing for healing.

In December 1997, Richard shared in a two-hour miracle service. During the second hour, the program was hooked up with several additional satellites and all their affiliated broadcast stations.

The power of God fell. Including the re-airing, we received more than 1,700 prayer requests on the phones, plus the many hundreds already sent by mail.

In addition to our prayer partners, Oral Roberts University's Prayer Tower received countless additional requests. We added the telephoned miracle reports together from Tulsa, Altoona, and Pittsburgh, and they totaled almost 200!

The Spirit of God had earlier told me that viewers would say, "I have never before seen healings like that on television!" One of those miracles should be told here.

Phyllis was suffering from heart disease, her liver was also diseased, and her kidneys had stopped functioning. In fact, a permanent shunt had been installed in her arm for dialysis.

When she learned about the healing service, Phyllis told the administrator of the nursing home where she lived, "I want to watch the program with Richard Roberts because God is going to heal me!"

"We can't receive Cornerstone here," the administrator—who was also a Christian—told Phyllis. "But let me see what I can do."

He phoned the station and talked with Gary Stewart.

"I think we have a solution," the administrator informed Phyllis. "Mr. Stewart at Cornerstone suggested that I could videotape the program at my home and then play it for you the next day."

"No," Phyllis replied, "I've got to see it *live*!"

That evening, just before the program with Richard Roberts aired, Phyllis suffered a massive heart attack and was rushed to the hospital, where she experienced a second heart attack. As her eyes rolled back, the staff thought she had died.

Suddenly, she showed signs of life and demanded, "Get me a television set!"

At her insistence, a television set was brought into the Intensive Care Unit! God made a way for Phyllis to watch *her* program—*live*!

When her doctor checked on her later, he was quoted as having said these words to Phyllis: "I can't understand it! I give you a clean bill of health! There is nothing wrong with your heart; there is nothing wrong with your kidneys; there is nothing wrong with your liver! I just don't understand it!"

Phyllis, however, knew exactly what had happened. "I watched the Richard Roberts program, and God healed me," she told the physician. "I'm only sorry I forgot to ask Him to heal my diabetes!"

We lost track of Phyllis after that, so we were unable to follow up on her miracles.

In addition, three of our Cornerstone employees were healed that most exciting evening!

Before the program ended, I had a vision, and I said, "Oral Roberts is watching at home in California. He is on the edge of his chair, and he is also pacing the floor—because God has given Oral a prophecy for the Body of Christ!"

Prayer Partners—The Heart of the Ministry

Within two minutes Oral was on the phone, and the studio audience broke out in loud applause.

Oral noted that I had described him perfectly, and he gave a wonderful prophecy that divine healing is again going to break out in the Church soon—"big time"!

I can hardly wait.

The home-diverter prayer partners often volunteer to stay up all night, if necessary, to answer calls. A few of them are house-bound.

One special couple, both of whom were paraplegics, had a very unique ministry. Each phone call required the two of them, working together, to complete the whole process—but they loved praying with needy people who called for help.

Carol McCarren lives not far from WPCB-TV. During our early days, she volunteered on the diverter every Tuesday night.

After midnight—about 1:00 a.m.—Carol's phone rang. The woman calling was a bit drunk and hysterical.

"My husband and my boys have walked out on me because of my drinking! I'm all alone in this 16-room mansion! I've got a gun, and I was about to kill myself when I heard a voice say, 'Look in your purse and call that number!' I found your number on a piece of paper in my purse! Please help me!"

Carol very patiently listened and talked to the woman who seemed to sober up quickly.

"My family is very wealthy, but I am miserable," she sobbed.

"Where do you live?" Carol asked.

"Boston"—the name of a little town just over the hill from Carol's home.

The conversation lasted four hours—until 5:00 a.m. Carol led the woman to the Lord. Then they prayed together and discussed how she could get her life together.

Finally, Carol had to have a break, and she asked, "What's your phone number? I'll call you right back."

"Oh no, that would be a long distance call. I'll phone *you*."

"But aren't you in Boston, Pennsylvania?"

"No, honey. I'm in Boston, Massachusetts!"

"Well, how did you get our number? This television station is in Pittsburgh."

"I don't know! I was in Pittsburgh recently, and maybe somebody gave it to me. I just heard a voice say, 'Look in your purse, and call that number!' And I did!"

Although that kind of miracle doesn't happen every day, it shows how the Spirit of God can work through our precious prayer partners.

Without our many volunteers the ministry of Cornerstone would not be effective. Most of them are prayer partners; many are intercessors; some have worked in our mailroom; others make trips to and from the airport. I have always loved working with volunteers.

Quite a few have themselves been healed through this ministry. It is not unusual for a prayer partner to receive a healing from a word of knowledge given on the air.

Prayer Partners—The Heart of the Ministry

One Thursday evening, Helen Mierski was on the prayer phone when I spoke a word about an elbow healing. Helen's phone rang just as she heard me give that word, and her very painful "tennis elbow" never hurt again.

Gil Rhodes, another regular on the phones, had been showing off on water skis and had injured his back severely. His wife wanted to take him to the hospital, but Gil said, "Nope! I'm going home, and the Lord's going to heal me!"

Gil arrived home, turned on the television set, and fell onto the couch in great pain. A few moments later he heard me say, during *Getting Together*, "God is healing someone in the back!"

Gil excitedly jumped off the couch—healed!

Eleanor Young does a lot of gardening and landscaping. Twice Eleanor contracted bad cases of poison ivy. Still, she came faithfully to answer the prayer phone, avoiding the other prayer partners, and carefully cleaning the telephone when she was finished.

Both times Eleanor returned home from Cornerstone with the rash and the itching gone!

God truly rewards our volunteers.

God has rewarded Norma and me miraculously, too.

During our early years on the air, Norma and I—and our family—lived on a salary of $16,000 a year, and we got along fine. The Lord can stretch money in remarkable ways—beyond our understanding.

Norma and I had learned that truth back in 1972. The Spirit of God had told me to give up my pastorate—my regular salary, my hospitalization, and my retirement—to step out on the deep water, trusting Him to provide. We enjoyed a six-year faith walk until I went on a small salary from the station in 1978.

Through most of those long nine years of planning and construction, I was strictly a volunteer. God miraculously provided for our family—except during one very difficult six-month period when Norma and I unknowingly dropped below the ten percent level of giving. I didn't realize it until income tax time the next April.

That was a very painful but significant lesson in the absolute importance of tithing. Trusting God for our personal finances and well-being has become "second nature" for Norma and me. For some years now, we have been giving about 20 percent—tithing twice!

Other personal miracles have occurred, too.

During one of the telethons, the producer asked me, as she normally did, "Choose the evening you and Norma would like to take off during the telethon."

"I don't know," I responded. "Just pick one."

So she did. At home during the very evening she had chosen for us, we heard a loud "bang!" in our basement, followed by the sound of rushing water. I ran downstairs and turned off the supply valve on our hot-water heating system, the water stopped, and minimal damage was done in our family room.

When the heating serviceman came right out to fix the pipe, I asked him, "What would have happened if we hadn't been at home this evening?"

"Well, for one thing, you'd probably have at least a foot of water in here. Everything on this floor would have been ruined."

That evening was our only time off during the telethon!

Norma and I *know* the truth of what Jesus said, "But seek first his kingdom and his righteousness, and all these [material] things shall be yours as well" (Matthew 6:33).

Chapter 13

Changing History Through Christian Television

Back in 1978, when we were struggling so hard to find the money to get on the air, God spoke to me about this most difficult problem: "Do you see how hard it is to raise the money you need without collateral? I want you to organize a nonprofit company that will lend money, without collateral, to budding Christian television stations like yours." And I did.

Six other CEOs like myself joined in the effort, and through the years Christian Television Services, Inc., has made interest-free loans to help put Christian stations on the air across the nation. This has been a most satisfying project during the past 20 or so years.

When the era of station-building ended, the Board of Directors of Christian Television Services, Inc., donated all its resources to the National Religious Broadcasters to help pay for the Television Wing of the NRB Museum in Manassas, Virginia.

Some years ago Oleen and I were discussing general facets of Christian television. I said, "Oleen, I think we should help these new stations in another way, too. I think we should offer to pay expenses for their key people to come here and learn television."

Oleen retorted, "Oh, Russ, nobody else does that! It's too expensive!"

Suddenly the words of Jesus from Mark 10:43 poured out of my mouth. Without thinking, I heard my voice say, "But it shall not be so among you!"

Oleen and I sat there in awe for a few minutes. We had a directive from God.

As a result, we have indeed helped a number of other stations get on the air, even to the point of sending our engineers to assist them. Expecting nothing but God's blessings in return, we give freely. After all, Jim Bakker did all this for us!

I n August 1983, our youngest son, John, left for college and presented me with the full responsibility of mowing the lawn. Our property is 200 feet deep, and some of it is rather steep.

As I mowed, I noticed that I would have to "take a break" about halfway through the lawn. This concerned me since I was only in my mid-50's.

Further, I have donated blood all my adult life—well over 125 times as of today. As a young man in my 20's, I would normally get out of the chair ahead of the donor who started giving blood before me. In my 30's I averaged the same length of time as the other blood donors.

In my 50's, however, I began to wonder what was wrong. One donor would finish before me; perhaps even two would pass me. "Isn't that bag full yet?" I'd ask the nurse.

"Oh, it's coming. Just a few more minutes."

I didn't realize what all this meant. I also had other little symptoms that I didn't recognize. I was headed for heart bypass surgery without knowing it.

One day in September 1983, Dr. Mary Ruth Swope, who used to teach nutrition at Ohio University, was our guest on *Getting Together*. Dr. Swope was talking about circulatory problems and how the arteries get clogged up around our hearts. She was selling a vitamin-mineral product that she suggested would help alleviate this problem.

"The difficulty," Dr. Swope pointed out, "is compounded by the fact that in 50 percent of the cases, the first symptom is *death*! We often have no warning; a vital artery clogs, and it's all over!"

I was quite bored with the interview; after all, I was already taking vitamins every day. Suddenly the Holy Spirit spoke in my heart: "You have the problem she's talking about, and I want you to buy what she's selling!"

Dr. Swope had my full attention immediately! I blurted out, "I want to talk to you when this program is over!"

Norma looked at me, wondering what had happened. I wrote out a check for the product as soon as the program ended. Dr. Swope was fascinated with the word I had received.

Within a brief time, I could mow the entire lawn without stopping. I can still do it today—in my 70's—without taking a break. I have, however, graduated to a self-propelled mower.

Two months after that program with Dr. Swope, I gave blood again. This time I got out of the chair *ahead* of the woman who was first in line. I hadn't experienced that in 30 years!

It still happens this way, more than 15 years later; I always pass at least one blood donor who starts immediately ahead of me. How I praise God for having mercy on me!

Dr. Swope later told us, "That program was the beginning of my nationwide ministry!" In gratitude she has sent our television ministry many contributions.

To this day, Norma and I take a similar but improved product every day; it's called Tru-Flow.

An additional blessing has been the effect on the health of many of our viewers.

One of my frustrations in the healing ministry had been to see people get healed by the Holy Spirit and then lose their healings three or four months later.

I began to realize that the problem was not what I usually suspected: "Is there somebody you haven't forgiven?" With a question like that I was usually putting a "guilt trip" on the person whose physical problem had returned.

The true problem, I have come to realize, is often environmental. Something in the person's lifestyle—either what he is eating, or what he is *not* eating, or both—has affected his (or her) health.

Maureen Salaman, one of the world's leading authorities on health and nutrition, began to appear regularly on *Getting Together,* talking enthusiastically about various nutritional products.

Getting Together gives healthy counsel. From left to right, Russ, Norma, Maureen Salaman, Dr. Francisco Contreras, Dr. Cal Streeter.

Folks started calling us to order these products, and Cornerstone TeleVision finally had to form a subsidiary called Optimum Health, later named Three Rivers Health and Nutrition. We receive great satisfaction in seeing thousands blessed by better health than they have experienced in many years.

I see divine healing and nutritional healing going hand in hand. In fact, the Bible is loaded with *both* emphases. We ignore biblical precepts at our own peril.

Now Cornerstone TeleVision has a health program of its own, *Nutritional Healing,* with Drs. Martin and Charlotte (Ciotti) Gallagher, two quite knowledgeable chiropractors with a large medical clinic in Jeannette, Pennsylvania.

Three Rivers Health and Nutrition needed a director to oversee the operation. As usual, Norma knew the person best suited for the job—Evelyn Kean, a longtime friend who had wanted to do whatever she could to help Cornerstone TeleVision.

From left to right: Tom Scott, Oleen Eagle, Evelyn Kean (director of Three Rivers Health and Nutrition), Russ.

Evelyn and her staff have fulfilled a great mission out of a store in Bridgeville, Pennsylvania. They occasionally hold a Saturday seminar with Maureen Salaman, or some other visiting medical and nutritional expert—and up to 500 people turn out.

We have received thousands of testimonies from Christians who tell how much healthier they are after using Three Rivers products.

As for myself, I have been amazed at the results of taking Vitamin C—which I call the "almost-a-miracle" vitamin. Another product that gives surprising results is one Maureen Salaman helped to develop, MineralRich. And of course, there is the Tru-Flow, which probably produces the greatest number of testimonies.

A relatively new product—CoEnzyme Q_{10}—has been thoroughly researched in Japan, and today most Japanese take it.

This enzyme has an amazing effect on damaged hearts, among other benefits.

Norma and I heard that one of our faithful volunteer drivers, 81-year-old Bill Malcomson, was dying of heart disease. Bill's doctor told Margaret to send for the children; his death was imminent.

Bill said, "Well, I don't want to die here in the hospital. Send me home." And the doctor reluctantly discharged Bill.

Norma and I made an immediate appointment to visit the Malcomsons. The atmosphere in their home was filled with fear and foreboding. We prayed for Bill and gave him a bottle of CoEnzyme Q_{10}.

Bill is now 86 years old and still driving! CoEnzyme Q_{10} is truly an amazing product; Norma and I take it regularly—just for protection.

Faithful volunteer driver Bill Malcomson preparing to leave on another airport run.

The road up our hill is steep—a 14 percent grade at its steepest—but we've always managed to keep it open in the winter.

"Superstorm '93" was the snowstorm of the century; 36 inches at our house and 48 inches at our son Paul's home, with WPCB-TV located between us.

As the storm stretched through the weekend, our snow plow operator worked for more than 48 hours, and we used a four-wheel drive to bring master control operators up and down the hill from Friday through Sunday—and WPCB-TV never went off the air. In fact, I personally have never missed a day of work because I couldn't drive up that steep hill.

Over the years, the half-mile-long dirt road had become filled with ruts. Some of our cars were being damaged, but we couldn't afford to pave the road.

A Christian contractor, Elwood Smith, phoned Ed Helmstadter, our facilities manager, one winter day. "I'll pave the worst part of the road if the station pays for the materials," he offered. "But I'll need warm weather for the asphalt."

That Saturday in February, God gave us a sunny winter day with the temperature an unseasonable 60 degrees!

Water presented another problem. We drilled a well on the hill, but the water was so polluted from earlier dumping that it was unfit for anything.

Our only other option was to build a cistern and have water trucked in—which we did for nearly 20 years. Still, we often experienced a water outage if the truck broke down or the pump at the cistern failed. Whenever a large group of people visited the station, our water supply would be quickly depleted.

To alleviate the problem we decided to ask our partners to contribute to a half-mile-long pipeline with a pumping station at the bottom of our hill. We knew that it would be an expensive

Digging the trench for the new water line.

and time-consuming project. In the end, however, the anticipated cost nearly doubled during construction.

When contributions for the water line reached the earlier announced goal, people still kept giving toward the project. Nearly double the budget was all paid for when the line was completed. The Lord knew all along how much it would cost!

In the summer of 1997, we finally enjoyed city water. Now we have all the water we need—and the local volunteer fire chief is relieved to know that we have a fire hydrant on top of the hill. The expensive water line was a godsend.

Cornerstone TeleVision has tried to be a good neighbor to the community. When our closest neighbors' home burned to the ground on Christmas Day 1994, the staff contributed liberally. When the water haulers' granddaughter drowned, we ministered to them. We contributed to a drug-education program in the local high school and annually give to the Borough of Wall, to the Wall Fire Department, and to the Rescue Squad.

Wall Borough is a small, old community whose population of 1,100 is only one-third of what it was during World War II. Today it is one of the poorest boroughs in Allegheny County.

The Borough Council has always been more than fair with us, and we have tried to reciprocate. The citizens of Wall Borough are proud that we chose their community to build WPCB-TV, and the feelings are mutual.

Joe Blazevich, President of the Wall Borough Council, told me in 1997, "I've lived here all my life, and I can say that Wall Borough has had nothing but good things happen since WPCB-TV came to our little town. We're the only borough in this valley that hasn't had to borrow any money, and all our bills are paid."

The secretary of the Wall Borough Council sent us this pleasant thank-you note after they received one of our gifts: "Thank you very much for the large donation. You people are the greatest. It will be used wisely as many things are needed at the [Borough] building. May the Lord bless all of you and thanks for keeping us in your prayers."

U nlike secular stations, Cornerstone TeleVision can more easily preempt scheduled programs in order to deal with urgent needs for prayer.

When President Ronald Reagan was shot in 1981, we repeatedly interrupted our scheduled programs, recruited a number of local pastors, and invited them to lead in prayer for the President's healing. We prayed much the same way during Operation Desert Storm in the Gulf War.

Changing History Through Christian Television

I've noticed how much power flows when we pray together on the air.

When our daughter Kathryn—who lived in Tulsa at the time—was facing gall bladder surgery, I led our viewers in prayer for her the evening before. The next morning, the surgeon removed a perfectly normal gall bladder.

The doctor was so angry he almost physically attacked the radiologist for giving him "false information"—until the radiologist handed the surgeon the previous day's X-rays, clearly showing one large gallstone.

Such stories have occurred again and again—when we all pray together—to the praise of Almighty God.

A most interesting story about professional baseball and hockey demonstrates this power of prayer on Christian television.

In 1987, I was watching the World Series between the St. Louis Cardinals and the Minnesota Twins. The Cardinals were easily the best team in all of baseball that season, and they handily defeated the Twins in the three games held in St. Louis.

During the four games in Minneapolis, "weird" things began happening to the Cardinals, and they lost all four games by close margins—and the World Series.

Norma does not care about sports, but she took an interest in what was happening as I called it to her attention. "Minneapolis," I told Norma, "is the 'witchcraft capital' of the United States, and the witches there are obviously cursing the Cardinals."

As I explained the strange occurrences, Norma also perceived it. Minneapolis is a fine city, with many Christians, and a number of Christians play on their baseball team. They didn't realize, however, what was occurring in the spiritual realm.

Four years later, in 1991, the Atlanta Braves had the best team in major league baseball; everybody knew it. They, too, were playing the Minnesota Twins in the World Series. Once again I mentioned the occult involvement and even got Norma to watch several of the games.

The seventh and final game in Minneapolis was scoreless in the late innings, and the Braves had a runner on first base. The Atlanta batter hit a long fly ball off the wall—almost a home run. The man on first base only had to run as fast as he could, and he would have scored the "go-ahead" and probably the winning run. As he rounded second base, he got confused and stopped momentarily. And that's as far as he got.

The Twins won on a fluke hit in the tenth inning, and the World Series was over! The witches won again!

Norma and I were fascinated—and disturbed—by this display of the powers of witchcraft.

"If only the Atlanta Braves were using their God-given discernment," I told Norma, "they could organize prayer against those curses in Minneapolis." Ironically, the Atlanta team was loaded with Christians.

We hadn't realized how that spiritual discernment would help just a few months earlier.

The Pittsburgh hockey team, the Penguins, had made it to the Stanley Cup finals the previous June. In the Western Division, a so-so team, the Minnesota North Stars, had a mediocre season, losing almost as many games as they won.

The witches, however, apparently got interested in the play-offs. On their way to the finals, these "mediocre" North Stars defeated the previous year's champions, the team with the second-best season record, and the team with the best season record—all three.

I told Norma, "We've got to take authority over the witches in Minneapolis. The North Stars are not a good team, yet they're beating everybody. Now they'll be playing the Pittsburgh Penguins in the Stanley Cup finals."

So Norma and I prayed.

Our prayers weren't having any effect. The Minnesota North Stars won two out of the first three games! The prospects looked bleak. Just as the fourth game was starting at 8:00 p.m., *Getting Together* was also beginning. Norma said, on the air, "Russell, I think we should pray for the Penguins."

I felt very strange about that. Does God care who wins the Stanley Cup?

Suddenly—I think it was from the Lord—I had an idea. I told the viewers, "The Pittsburgh Penguins are now playing the Minnesota North Stars in hockey. Obviously you don't care about hockey, or you wouldn't be watching this channel. I don't think God cares who wins this hockey game either, but He does care about what the devil is doing. Minneapolis is the witchcraft capital of America, and those witches are cursing the Penguins. The Minnesota Twins won the 1987 World Series because of those curses. Now!—let's show the devil that 'He who is in you is greater than he who is in the world.' Everybody! Let's agree together!

"Satan, I bind your activities in those hockey games, in Jesus' name! I neutralize any curses coming against the Penguins! And we loose both teams from any demonic activity, so the better team may win! In Jesus' name! Amen!"

I opened my eyes and saw Dale, the Floor Director. He was grinning. He held up a finger. "One goal!" Dale shouted. Somebody at our station was following the game and reporting it over Dale's headset.

Before Norma and I could get on with the program, he held up two fingers: "Two goals!" he exploded.

Within seconds, a third finger went up. "Three goals!" Dale yelled.

Three goals in just several minutes! It was an instant turnaround!

The Pittsburgh Penguins won that evening by a big score; the next game was a victory, too; and the final game was eight to nothing, Pittsburgh!

The 1991 Penguins won the Stanley Cup in WPCB-TV's studio, and they didn't even know it! Such is the power we all have over the devil when we are in total agreement.

Christian television is just "scratching the surface" of the possibilities for serving the Kingdom of God. Every one of us should learn an important lesson from this incident!

One day in 1986, a man phoned our facilities manager, Ed Helmstadter. "My name is Roy, and I would like to volunteer to do maintenance work for the station."

Ed was thrilled. No one had ever volunteered to do such dirty, hard, boring work.

Roy's life, however, was in turmoil—as Ed soon learned.

In 1977, Roy and his wife Sandy had made commitments to Jesus and become actively involved—along with their five children—in a local church. Previously, most of their evenings had been spent drinking at a local bar as well as drinking at home. Roy had been gambling, too.

Gradually, Roy and Sandy drifted away from the Lord and began living the old life again. More and more Roy stayed away from home, ignoring his wife and their children.

Feeling unloved and neglected, Sandy—out of loneliness and depression—became friendly with a male co-worker who sympathized and filled her emptiness. Eventually, she found herself out of state with this other man, away from her family and away from God.

Roy admitted to us that it was mostly his fault; he had been an indifferent husband and was dating another woman. He was disgusted with himself.

Instead of venting his anger, Roy reached out to the Lord. Hurt and lonely, he still longed for his wife, the mother of his children.

Roy would talk to us frankly about his wife's affair, asking all of us again and again, "Pray that she will return home."

Week after week Roy would proclaim, "I know God's going to bring her back to us. Please pray!"

About every two months, Sandy would return to Pittsburgh to visit her wounded children. She began to notice the difference in Roy; he was so gentle, not at all like the man she had married.

The prayers were working; Sandy soon became disillusioned with her new companion and finally asked Roy if he would take her back.

Roy was ecstatic! "Jesus has made the difference," he explained to Sandy. "Jesus is the One who brought you home."

Sandy recommitted her life to the Lord, too.

Roy couldn't speak highly enough of the staff at Cornerstone, so Sandy also began to volunteer and later came on staff full-time.

One Friday morning in our 9:00 a.m. Bible study, the power of God sovereignly fell on Sandy. "I felt as if somebody poured a bucketful of love all over me!" she told us later. "I wanted to hug everybody!"

Sandy began speaking in tongues and rejoicing as Jesus baptized her in the Holy Spirit. Our entire staff was excited about the change in her.

"I know God has truly accepted me in spite of my sin," Sandy exclaimed. "I feel so clean!" The power of the Holy Spirit surging through her confirmed the forgiveness that Sandy had felt unworthy to receive from God.

Being baptized in the Spirit provides every believer with a continuing awareness of the risen Lord Jesus Christ.

Roy and Sandy DaVane, happy at their daughter's wedding.

Changing History Through Christian Television

Suddenly Sandy was smiling all the time. When she finished one job, she'd look for another—helping in the mailroom, washing dishes for the *At Home* set, entering data on the computers for the Partner Services Department. Sandy is one of our hardest-working employees, and she's always warm and encouraging to everyone.

One problem still troubled Sandy—she couldn't stop smoking. Many of us prayed with her, but she'd always have a struggle until she lit another cigarette. Then, in January of 1997, Jesus set her free, and Sandy hasn't had a cigarette since.

Earlier, not long after they were reunited, Roy and Sandy received frightening news: Roy had a serious, fast-growing type of cancer in his leg. This cancer almost always requires amputation, often followed by further amputation, or even death.

One morning before Roy and Sandy were to leave for a noted cancer hospital in Buffalo, they came by the station for prayer first. About a dozen of our staff surrounded them in the chapel, and everyone sensed that something wonderful was happening. Others who prayed with them also assured Roy that his leg would be all right.

Today, Roy still has that leg! God is so good!

People who knew Roy and Sandy during their bar-hopping days cannot believe the dramatic transformation in them—all because of Jesus!

Norma and I rejoice when we realize that the staff at Cornerstone TeleVision is practicing what we preach.

S teve Totin, who for years had been coordinator of the prayer partners, began to correspond with prisoners in various penitentiaries who had contacted him. Although Steve was having notable success ministering to them, initially he was not particularly drawn to working with inmates. This ministry just seemed to seek him out.

An angry letter came in one day's mail. "There is no God! And you people are a bunch of thieves, promising that if I plant a $1,000 seed, God will bless my business financially! It's all a scam! Look what it got me!"

Since the letter came from a prison, it was referred to Steve Totin. Steve wrote to this angry inmate a response in the same tone: "The problem with you is that you haven't matured as a Christian. You've always bullied your way through life, and now you're in jail for abusing your wife. You need to begin confessing God's Word if you want your business to prosper. The Word of God needs to come alive in you."

Several months later our switchboard operator nervously called Steve. Arriving in the lobby, Steve encountered a stocky, angry-looking man: "Are you the one who wrote me this letter?" he demanded.

Steve recognized his stationery from a distance. He looked at the letter, and said, "Yeah, I wrote it."

"I just came here to thank you," responded the gruff voice. "All my life I've bullied everybody. You're the first person who ever told me the truth about myself, and it's changed my life! Since I got out of jail, I've been doing what you said, and my business has taken off. I can't even keep up with it! That seed-planting really works!"

Steve Totin just has a "way" with prisoners. By the time that incident occurred, half of Steve's workday already involved prison ministry. The answer was obvious: Steve needed to do this work full-time.

In 1997, Steve's job description was changed. God had a tailor-made ministry for Steve Totin and Cornerstone TeleVision.

Changing History Through Christian Television

Occasionally Steve takes a camera crew into a maximum-security prison, and they come out with some great testimonies on video.

Every Christmas Steve Totin and his family and friends purchase hundreds of children's gifts. Each one is wrapped and mailed as if it came from a father or a mother in prison. Often it is the only Christmas gift that child receives.

Cornerstone TeleVision continues to change history—one life at a time.

I love maps. Sometimes I will sit and stare at a map for an hour, memorizing much that I see. I have a small collection of maps and atlases.

One day I picked up an old *National Geographic* map of the "Megalopolis"—the area roughly from Boston to Washington, D.C. where one out of eight Americans lives. That corridor is like a very large city; thus its name, the Megalopolis, which means "very large city."

I had seen that map a number of times before, but when I opened it this time, I spontaneously began to cry over it. I could see millions of people from the Megalopolis going to hell.

I quickly recalled two events. First, the time in February of 1981 when the Holy Spirit had quickened the words "regional ministry" so prominently. Second, the time when Jesus cried over the city of Jerusalem.

I knew—although I didn't know how—we had to reach the Megalopolis, the one major area of our nation with minimal access to Christian television. I received those tears as a directive from the Lord Jesus Himself!

I also recalled David Wilkerson's story of how he began to cry when he saw the magazine picture of several Brooklyn boys who had committed a gang murder. It was David's personal call to found the divinely inspired Teen Challenge in Brooklyn.

We must reach the Megalopolis with the gospel!

T he Philadelphia station, Channel 48, located in the heart of the Megalopolis, created an opportunity—and a problem.

Cornerstone TeleVision owned the station, but that didn't mean we could broadcast on it. We needed a license from the FCC, but others had also applied. To make matters worse, we had two strikes against us.

First, the FCC favors applicants who have no other broadcast interests; Cornerstone TeleVision already owned WPCB-TV in Pittsburgh and WKBS-TV in Altoona. Second, the FCC also prefers women and minorities. One applicant was a small group of women, and another was an African-American woman from Baltimore. A third applicant was Sinclair Broadcasting, also from Baltimore. In addition to Cornerstone TeleVision, a number of others had applied for the FCC license—in spite of the fact that *we* owned the equipment!

After several years of protracted bureaucratic wrangling, the lady from Baltimore—who had most of what the Commission sees as "pluses"—received the Construction Permit from the FCC. Sinclair Broadcasting challenged the decision as long as they could in Federal Court, trying to bleed her dry, but she hung on.

We knew that this lady would have to deal with us; after all, our station (minus the transmitter, which had been moved to

Altoona) was sitting right there waiting for her. We met for lunch, and she brought her pastor, who spoke about her in glowing terms.

Dedicating Channel 48, Philadelphia, to the Lord.

"That's great!" we exclaimed, excited that we'd be working with a Christian.

"We'd like to trade some air time for part of your rent payment," we told her. "At least we'll have a few hours to air gospel programs in Philadelphia."

She agreed. Although we tried to do everything we could to help her get on the air, most of the time she told us, "I'm taking care of the matter."

But things didn't work out as we had anticipated. "My Nielsen ratings go down every time your programs come on," she stated.

"How can that be?" we wondered. "During telethons we are getting an increasing response from Philadelphia."

We were getting nowhere, so I finally told Oleen, "I think we should pray and ask God to sell the station—to anybody!"

Eventually we sold the station to this lady. We ended up making a small profit on the sale, but it certainly wasn't worth all the problems.

What grieved us most was abandoning those wonderful viewers in Philadelphia—many of whom had accepted Jesus during those several years we were on the air in that city. In fact, we had come to love them so much that I actually found myself cheering for the Phillies (unheard of in Pittsburgh)!

We are praying that someday Cornerstone TeleVision will be able to share the gospel again in Philadelphia. We must persist in working to reach the Megalopolis before Jesus returns.

Chapter 14

Expanding the Outreach

"The Lord instructed me to build a low-power television station to provide a northern translator station for WPCB-TV."

When Scott Krepps, a shy young draftsman who lived north of Pittsburgh, told me that one day, I didn't know what to say.

As he set out to obey the Lord, we were all amazed at this young man's quiet confidence in his vision. Scott filed his application at the FCC (with our counsel), worked to find a location, helped to raise the money, and then turned it over to us to do the actual construction.

The new station—W50BF, located in Hermitage, Pennsylvania, near Youngstown, Ohio—provides an extension of Cornerstone's signal into an area where WPCB-TV's signal is weak. In addition, Don Reed, an accountant in Hermitage, has worked to get our signal on the local cable systems.

Jack Reitz of Brookville, Pennsylvania, was another quiet man of faith. Many years ago the Lord had told Jack to go to Africa as a missionary. With his age and a heart condition working against him, no mission agency would accept him.

Channel 50 of Hermitage, Pennsylvania. From left to right: Russ, Norma, Scott Krepps, Donna Reed, Don Reed.

Without official sanction and having very limited finances, Jack Reitz went to Africa, where he served until he retired. After he and Margaret returned home to Brookville, the Lord told Jack to build a low-power translator station for WPCB-TV.

With our assistance, Jack raised the finances from his community, then asked Christian friends, Harry and Ann Watt, to allow the transmitter to be put on their hill. As W51AO repeats our signal over an area northeast of Pittsburgh, Harry still faithfully monitors the transmitter and drives to the city for repairs when necessary.

After Channel 51 went on the air, Jack and Margaret Reitz were admiring the twinkling red tower lights one evening.

"I've now completed everything God told me to do," Jack told his wife with satisfaction. Several days later Jack quietly went home to celebrate with his wonderful Lord, leaving a glorious legacy.

Late one night Ron Deitrich—a disabled truck driver who lives in the Allegheny Mountains west of Harrisburg, Pennsylvania—was flipping through the channels on his television set. With few options available back in the mountains, he was surprised to locate WKBS-TV, Channel 47, our Altoona station. Ron finally found television worth watching!

"Bette!" he called out, "look what I found!" and they sat up nearly all night, soaking up the anointed Christian programing.

"I've got to find out where that Christian station is located!" he told his wife.

When he went to his neighbors' homes, he discovered that no one else in those hollows could pick up Channel 47!

Ron Deitrich persisted, and he finally contacted us.

Ron and Bette Deitrich (right) of Elliottsburg, Pennsylvania, with an unknown friend (Channels 12 and 18).

Unlike our two quiet and reserved visionaries in Hermitage and Brookville, Ron bubbled with enthusiasm. "We've just got to get Christian television in Perry County! Help me reach my neighbors with the gospel!"

Ron followed through and received the Construction Permit for low-power Channel 12. Several years later, Ron applied for and received the Permit for low-power Channel 18 in Snyder County, some distance to the north. Both stations are spreading the Good News from Superstation WPCB-TV to the Susquehanna River area today because a disabled truck driver had a burden to reach the lost.

These three ordinary men, with their faithful wives, have been able to accomplish more for the Kingdom of God than most Christians ever dream of!

T he Spirit of God sovereignly chose Oleen Eagle that day in 1976 when Norma placed a check mark beside Oleen's name. (Norma often knows in her spirit which particular Christian is supposed to do a certain job.)

Always eager to accept a challenge, Oleen learned television on the job. An excellent manager, Oleen—like Norma—has good sense about people and knows how to delegate responsibility. As a result, God has given us a great team of committed experts to fill the various positions at Cornerstone TeleVision.

When visitors tell me, "You have such a dedicated and talented staff," I almost always get tears in my eyes.

I sometimes reply—if not orally, at least mentally to myself: "Because I'm a visionary—and I usually have my head in the clouds—I might have bankrupted this ministry had I tried to run the daily operations."

Oleen, on the other hand, has her feet on the ground; together the two of us make a good team.

I've been told that I have a gift for believing the Lord for something that's never been done before. Then, after God brings it to pass, Oleen makes it work efficiently.

The day-to-day management of Cornerstone TeleVision revolves around Oleen Eagle's unusual combination of administrative skills and spiritual depth.

One day in 1988 Oleen sensed a leading by God to phone Ron Hembree, who by that time had been senior pastor of that huge congregation in Rockford, Illinois, for several years. By any standard, Ron's ministry there had been quite successful.

"But," he told Oleen on the phone, "I feel called to television."

"The door is wide open," Oleen responded.

When Ron arrived in Pittsburgh, he almost fell apart. His wife had been seeing another man, and Ron knew that he had to get her out of Rockford. When she refused to leave, he came to Pittsburgh alone—and brokenhearted.

Ron Hembree of *Project '90*, 1988.

231

The entire staff at WPCB-TV began to demonstrate their love for Ron. Although he refused to divorce his wife, she finally divorced him.

Just being able to minister on television had a healing effect on Ron. He received a lot of personal well-wishes and prayers from viewers—especially from many of the pastors who knew him.

In his grief, Ron Hembree poured himself into his work with abandon. Always energetic, he tried to stay busy every minute of his life. He hardly ever ate more than one full meal a day.

When a friend's ministry needed a vehicle, Ron donated his Jeep and drove it across the country as a favor. On the way, Ron stopped in Phoenix to renew several acquaintances and had breakfast with Cathy, who had been a member of Ron's church years before.

As Ron left Phoenix and drove on to California, the Lord spoke to him: "I have given you your wife!"

Ron and Cathy have made a wonderful pair, more recently adopting four older children, each child having a spectacular testimony.

We started a daily program for Ron, called *His Place*–"the diner show," but it didn't seem to be Ron's niche.

After returning from a national conference focused on 1990 as the Year of the Bible, Oleen enthusiastically approached Ron: "Why don't you consider teaching through the Bible for a year, five days a week."

The program, first called *Project '90,* was an immediate success, and Ron sensed that this was to be his life's work.

Within two years, Project '90 became such a big production that "the tail began wagging the dog," and Ron knew he'd have to move on. We all knew that what he wanted to do with his concept was too big for Cornerstone at that time.

Today, Ron produces *Life Lessons* both in Phoenix and in Toronto. Ron's two natural children, Rod and Robin, have become extremely talented additions to the program, carried weekdays on Cornerstone and now called *Quick Study*.

Although he no longer ministers in our Pittsburgh studio, we still think of Ron Hembree as part of this ministry.

I n her original vision in August of 1969, the Spirit of God had told Norma that He would raise up the people we needed from the community.

When a young man from our local area, Tim Burgan, came to us with a college education in television production, we quickly realized that he could also do other things well.

Since Ron Hembree didn't seem to "click" on *His Place*, Oleen asked Tim, "Would you try it for a while? At least until the Lord raises up somebody else."

As the very capable "proprietor," Tim has helped boost the popularity of *His Place* across the nation. The E-mail received by *His Place* has been phenomenal, as this viewer's note indicates: "I live in North Carolina and watch your program on a local access cable channel that broadcasts religious television. Even though I'm a fervent agnostic, I find your program a fascinating culmination [sic] of the Christian religion. You guys are definitely interesting to watch in action."

After a reporter from a Pittsburgh newspaper appeared as a guest on *His Place* one evening, two of his agnostic co-workers challenged him the next day: "What were you doing on that religious television station last night?"

Jeff Redinger, Andrea Hopkins, Robin Heiple, and Tim Burgan of *His Place.*

"What were you doing watching it?" he retorted.

Thom and Cathy Hickling, Tim Burgan, Robin Heiple, Andrea Hopkins, and Jeff Redinger have made a great team of enthusiastic young people, translating that energy into a well-received program.

My favorite *His Place* program involved Ginger Ault, who played the role of Millie—a waitress, a single mom of troubled teenagers, and a dabbler in New Age religion.

Pregnant "out-of-wedlock," Millie "had an abortion." On the program, she told a friend about the horror of the experience and how the abortion clinic personnel had lied to her.

Then the picture switched to a pre-produced insert in which Ginger tells young women how to get the pro-life help they need during an unwanted pregnancy.

Expanding the Outreach

It was one of the most dramatic television programs I've ever seen. That particular program—along with others—has impacted the lives of many viewers.

Andrea and Jeff remembered one couple, Julie and Steve, whose lives were dramatically affected by the ministry of *His Place.*

Sexually abused as a child, Julie brought severe problems into her marriage. When her husband Steve became physically abusive, Julie had to get a "protection from abuse" order from the court.

One day, while Steve was at work, Julie took their three daughters and left. Allowed only six hours on Saturdays with the girls (and a chaperon), Steve was devastated by the loss of his family. To make matters worse, Julie would close the door in his face as he picked up his daughters for their weekly visits. Soon Julie decided to divorce Steve.

With their lives in turmoil, both were seeing psychologists. Julie's lawyer insisted that she meet with Steve's psychologist before he would proceed with the divorce.

At the same time, Julie and Steve separately began attending church. The members of both congregations started taking an interest in their situation.

Steve began to pray that God would restore their marriage, and Julie went to the altar every Sunday to pray about her future.

In the midst of their difficulties, Julie and Steve separately found Cornerstone TeleVision. Steve especially enjoyed watching *His Place* every evening.

Whenever the guests on the program told how God had restored their marriages, Steve would record *His Place* on his

VCR. "Ask your mom to watch this," he would suggest to his daughters.

Unimpressed, Julie told herself, "Once an abuser, always an abuser." Yet her daughters were telling their mother, "Daddy is different!"

Steve began phoning the prayer partners at Cornerstone, asking God for the miracle he so desperately wanted.

The next Saturday morning, Steve realized that the Holy Spirit had already been at work. The girls came out to his car carrying a large bag. Inside were all the foods Julie knew Steve liked to eat.

Soon they met for the first time with a Christian counselor, and Julie suddenly realized that she still had her original feelings for Steve.

After a Christian counseling session, the two talked privately for several hours. They decided to try again—this time with Jesus at the center of their relationship. After one night together, Julie was amazed at the change Jesus had made in Steve.

Every evening, the two watched *His Place*. They especially related to the characters of Jeff and Meredith, who were working through their relationship problems. Steve and Julie repeatedly looked at each other and agreed: "That's us!" By watching Jeff and Meredith they learned how to communicate.

Through Cornerstone TeleVision, and *His Place* in particular, Jesus healed a broken marriage! This beautiful story demonstrates how the local church and Christian television ministry reinforce each other.

Oleen enjoys working closely with the *His Place* crew, critiquing almost mercilessly while seeking to draw the creativity out of "her" young people. The drama's actors and actresses take her counsel and run with it.

Oleen is so proud of that team! They spend a great deal of time in "character development," bringing new characters into the drama as often as seems appropriate. Keeping the program fresh and interesting while always focused on the ultimate purpose—evangelism—remains a constant challenge.

When David Plisé—a truck driver in northern California from a little town called Klamath River—developed a tumor in his neck in 1994, his life took a dramatic turn. To cope, David stayed drunk.

Although he and his live-in girlfriend Amy constantly argued, she loved David enough to stay with him.

As David's tumors began to spread, they became desperate for help. They found a small church where David committed his life to Jesus Christ, and Amy, who had walked away from the Lord many years before, recommitted her life. The two married, and their pastor began to minister to the Plisé family.

The cancerous tumors continued to grow, and David underwent four operations for melanoma. After the medical treatments, the doctors gave David six months to live.

David's social worker told him about Dalmation Dreams, a charitable organization (similar to Make-a-Wish foundation for children) that provides a final wish for terminally ill adults.

In his letter to Dalmation Dreams, David requested, "We would like to [appear] as guests on the Christian television program, *His Place*. It is very important to me to express my love and gratitude to the Lord in this way, so that others may gain strength in facing trials such as mine....This experience would give my wife and daughters the memory that I would like them to have of me and my faith in Jesus...My time with my family is growing short...."

In early 1998, Dalmation Dreams phoned Tim Burgan and made the arrangements. United Airlines flew David and Amy—along with their two children—free, to and from Pittsburgh. Holiday Inn of Monroeville, Pennsylvania, provided two free rooms.

David's condition required special care, and everyone was happy to help. Because of his weakness, the trip required five days.

David, Amy, and the girls received a lot of love at Cornerstone TeleVision. By the time they arrived in Pittsburgh, two of David's six months had already passed.

The Plisés shared on *Getting Together* as well as *His Place*, where Tim Burgan asked all the viewers to pray for David.

When we realized the impact of the SkyAngel satellite—touching a family in rural northern California so powerfully that David's only wish was to share his salvation testimony on *His Place*—we were all thrilled. David "graduated" in April 1998, joyful to the end.

I n 1981, David Mainse of *100 Huntley Street* in Canada invited Norma and me to be on his program.

Norma was quite taken with the musicians ministering that day, Dean and Mary Brown. When she asked if they'd be willing to sing on our struggling station in Pittsburgh, the Browns accepted immediately.

Expanding the Outreach

Dean and Mary Brown reading pledges.

Dean and Mary were some of our first guests in the new studio.

The Lord soon spoke to both Oleen and Norma that the Browns should do a regular program on our station. Oleen taught them how to produce their television program.

Music That Ministers began in 1985, and today it is carried on nearly every Christian station in the United States and is seen around much of the world. Dean and Mary continue to change lives through their faith-building ministry of music and worship.

One segment of *Music That Ministers* took an unusual turn. Cameraman Ray Heiple had a surprise for the girl who used to work on the next camera, Robin Helmstadter (Ed and Martha Helmstadter's niece). The two had been dating for a while.

In a pre-arranged, on-air scene of the Dean and Mary show, Ray came onto the set and popped the question, "Robin, will you marry me?"

The camera dramatically caught a tear flowing down Robin's cheek as she replied, "Yes."

Ray and Robin Heiple on their wedding day.

Everybody at Cornerstone knew the plans except Robin, and the entire staff was watching on their television monitors. Dean and Mary had a glorious time orchestrating the entire event.

Tom McGough, a baseball pitcher who came up through the minor leagues to the Cleveland Indians, began working for Cornerstone TeleVision in 1993. Tom had a no-hit game to his credit in the AA league, with a 98-mile-an-hour fastball.

Expanding the Outreach

Tom, of course, loves sports, but he loves Jesus even more. Using his baseball background as a platform, Tom speaks at Christian churches and meetings two or three times a week.

Tom had an idea for a program called *Sportsweek*, where he and other professional athletes report and comment on the week's major league sporting events. Then an athlete shares his Christian testimony.

Tom McGough of *Sportsweek*.

Sportsweek caught on quickly, as many stations across the country realized its benefit as an evangelistic tool. Even a few secular stations carry it.

Every Tuesday evening, *Sportsweek* attracts a large number of nonbelievers. At the same time, the regular viewers realize how many young professional athletes are born-again Christians.

Over the years, we have developed various types of programs in an effort to strengthen the entire Body of Christ and to reach varied groups with the message of salvation.

When Tom Green came to us from the *PTL Club* in 1982, he brought along his passion for every kind of music—from longhair to country and from rock 'n' roll to waltzes. After Tom developed a program called *Lightmusic,* the format evolved into mostly contemporary Christian music.

Tom Green of *Lightmusic*.

Although our older viewers would prefer more sedate music, I have always stood by Tom (and his program) for one reason: the mail. Numerous young people have written to say they were weaned from MTV and into the Kingdom of God through *Lightmusic.* A special aspect of this ministry has been the averting of potential youthful suicides.

The winner of numerous national awards, *Lightmusic* has had its place on television as we try to reach all segments of the population with the gospel.

Expanding the Outreach

In 1997, Tom Green sensed a call to move to New Zealand to work for a new Christian television network there. Cornerstone TeleVision has also helped this overseas ministry with counsel and with finances.

Bob Anderson, a former sports announcer and another former employee of the *PTL Club,* worked with us for a time. When Bob became interested in studying cults and occultism, he was often asked to speak in churches about this growing spiritual problem.

We felt that Bob should teach the subject on Cornerstone TeleVision, and he developed a very enlightening program called *Exposing the Lie.* Countless viewers have had their eyes opened to false religions through Bob's teachings and interviews on *Exposing the Lie.*

Seminar speaker Ray Mossholder of Phoenix, Arizona, occasionally appeared on *Getting Together.* During one of those appearances, the Spirit of God told me that Ray was to do a regular weekly program on Cornerstone TeleVision.

For many years, his ministry has centered around helping to heal broken marriages. More recently, Ray has also been ministering effectively to singles.

Finally, after some years of planning, *Marriage Plus* and *Singles Plus* were inaugurated in 1997. Both programs were immediately successful.

Ray and Arlyn Mossholder on a telethon.

Ray is truly an anointed teacher, and our own Mark Grover and Paul McDonald, who share prominent leadership roles in both shows, brought quality to the programs.

Lorraine Williams, a leader in the African-American Christian community who used to work for Prison Fellowship, hosts a well-received women's program called *Let's Talk*, which was first hosted by Oleen.

Oleen Eagle with guest Louise Norris on *Let's Talk*.

Expanding the Outreach

Abraham and Eve Fenton, originally from Trinidad, who today are co-pastors of a thriving congregation in New Jersey, host a fine teaching program called *Living By the Word.*

Abraham and Eve Fenton of Willingboro, New Jersey, on *Living By the Word.*

In June 1992, psychologist Kevin Leman of Tucson, Arizona, appeared on *Getting Together.* On radio for years, Dr. Leman has a winsome, humorous style of teaching family values.

That evening the Lord told me that Dr. Leman was to do a regular weekly show on Cornerstone TeleVision. I promptly spoke the word of the Lord to Kevin, and we agreed to pray about the matter.

Finally, more than six years later, in late 1998, Dr. Leman's delightful new program, *Real Families,* produced in our studio, began to be seen on Cornerstone TeleVision. Sometimes a word from God is slow in arriving, but, as we're told in Habakkuk 2:3,

For still the vision awaits its time; it hastens to the end—it will not lie. If it seem slow, wait for it; it will surely come, it will not delay.

Steve McVey of Atlanta, an author and convention speaker, does a weekly program called *Grace Walk*. Steve also hosts *Getting Together* on an occasional basis.

During the first eight months of 1998, *six* of Cornerstone TeleVision's programs won eight national, secular awards—eight awards!—for *Getting Together, His Place, Marriage Plus* (two), *Singles Plus* (two), *Sportsweek*, and *At Home With Arlene Williams*. In January 1999, we won *three more awards*—for *Getting Together, Sportsweek*, and *Marriage Plus*.

Cornerstone TeleVision receiving the Award of Merit, National Religious Broadcasters Convention, 1985. Dr. Brandt Gustavson and Dr. Bob Cook presenting. (Photo credit: Ken Deata and Tim Bandy.)

All those awards led to Cornerstone TeleVision's receiving the "Television Station Award for 1999" from the National Religious Broadcasters!

Expanding the Outreach

In earlier years, *Music That Ministers* and *Lightmusic* also won national awards. How we praise God for what He's doing at Cornerstone!

And still *more* good programs are on the drawing boards.

P ain and sickness have always been frustrating for me. When I was pastor of the Pittsburgh Church of the Brethren, I hated to see people whom I loved suffering.

Most pastors develop a "professional" style of dealing with these problems, but I never could be smooth or artificial. I dealt with sickness rather awkwardly.

After Norma and I were baptized in the Spirit in 1967, however, I could hardly wait to get my hands on people who were hurting. God began healing them one after another.

One day I was talking casually to Tibb Gethin, the remarkable lady who had led Norma to the Lord. Suddenly, she sat up straight in her chair, "Russ! The Lord says this scripture is for you!" Then she began to quote Isaiah 61:1. "That's your ministry, Russ!"

I was so excited that I went home and translated it from the Hebrew for myself. I suspected that these verses had some supernatural qualities that noncharismatic translators might have missed. Here is my translation.

The Spirit of the Lord God has been placed upon me, because the Lord has anointed me; He has sent me to bring good news to the suffering, to heal hearts that are broken, to proclaim to captives release from slavery, and freedom to those who are in bondage.

That precious verse of scripture has indeed characterized my ministry ever since.

Prior to 1967 we had seen a few healing miracles, but not nearly enough to suit me. I hated to see someone die before his or her time.

After receiving the Holy Spirit that year, Norma and I watched God heal our congregation. A number of years passed before anyone who regularly attended our church died. We had learned—both from scripture and from actual experience—that it's God's will to heal the sick!

I brought this hatred of pain and sickness into television. I *love* to see the Holy Spirit heal His people!

Richard Roberts' spectacular daily healing program, *Something Good Tonight,* began in the fall of 1997. We are delighted to carry it on Cornerstone TeleVision and have encouraged Richard in this ministry. Many people are healed every evening.

Occasionally the thought runs through my mind, *Is anyone really watching?* Then I read a letter such as the one I received from Rose.

Dr. Rose Sims of Ridge Manor, Florida, was an educator and pastor. After her pastor-husband died, Rose was called to the leadership of a United Methodist congregation. Located in a poverty-stricken community, the church had several strikes against it. In spite of the handicaps, the congregation grew spectacularly, and most of the new members had not been Christians earlier.

Today Rose Sims is very much in demand, traveling the nation and speaking frequently on television and radio and at churches and pastors' conferences.

Expanding the Outreach

After she appeared on *Getting Together,* Rose wrote this thank-you note: "The response to this telecast was overwhelming. More orders of books, more phone calls than any TV show I've done. Are you going to rerun it ever? The need for churches to come back to Jesus is enormous."

It looks as if people are watching!

Chapter 15

Financial Miracles Work Both Ways

At one point, when Cornerstone was hurting financially, I called our contact person at CBN. "Would you consider raising—at least a little bit—the amount CBN pays Cornerstone TeleVision for our carrying *The 700 Club* twice a day?"

"I'll get back to you," he replied.

A few days later this CBN executive returned the call, offering to pay us—not an increase—but only *half* of what they had been paying. "And after two more years," he said, "we won't pay you anything."

I was incensed. "Do you want us to drop *The 700 Club*?"

"Oh, no! But that's all we can afford." CBN was having some financial problems, too.

I blasted him for being so callous to us smaller ministries. "I'll get back to you, but don't expect us to take this lying down!"

Oleen, Jim Fitzgerald, and David Skeba met with me. David and Jim wanted to knuckle under to the reduction in payments. Oleen was on the fence. But I was deeply angered.

I almost yelled, "Absolutely not!" I was furious.

In the midst of my rantings, the Spirit of Jesus spoke in my spirit: "I don't want you to accept their offer. I want you to *give* CBN the air time—free!" Then He added, "If anyone strikes you on the right cheek, turn to him the other also."

Suddenly my face flushed; I stopped my raving and blurted out what I had just heard. I was laughing and crying at the same time as the result of the violent change in emotions.

Blake Richert working on a videotape recorder with Cindy Chester assisting.

Financial Miracles Work Both Ways

Not one to accept something just because a person states it emphatically, Oleen was so awed by my sudden change that she knew it had to be from God. She was speechless. In fact, no one could argue.

"Russ!" exclaimed David. "You just went from here to here!"—swinging his arm in a 180-degree arc.

"I know! I know! Now God has to make up all the money we're losing!"

He did.

After a couple of years of *The 700 Club's* free television time on our station, David Skeba began asking me if we could start charging CBN for the air time once again.

I kept putting him off, saying, "I'll pray about it."

After about five of his requests, I got a bright idea—although I think the Spirit put it in my heart. "My secretary Irene knows nothing about this matter, and she can hear from God. Let's ask Irene to pray about it."

So David and I explained—as briefly as we could so as not to prejudice her prayer—to Irene about our request for a word from God. Then we all prayed together.

Within a minute or so, Irene responded, "The Lord says, 'I have already told you what to do.' "

And David has never brought up the subject again!

Oleen saw clearly our desperate need for more work-space. We needed larger facilities for ministry; we needed more office and storage space; and our producers/directors were clamoring for better production facilities.

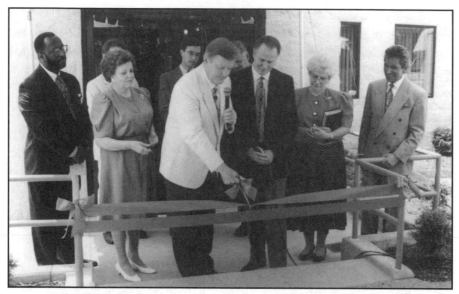

Russ and Richard Roberts dedicating Stage One of the Isaiah 54 project. Behind are, from left to right: Dr. Mitchel Nickols, David Skeba (behind), Norma, Tom Scott, Blake Richert, Oleen Eagle, Stan Scott.

For several years, Oleen's prayer was, "New facilities without debt. Without debt, Lord."

God gave Oleen her request. We dedicated the first phase of the "Isaiah 54 Project" in July of 1995—without debt.

It was quite a financial miracle since we were always short of operational funds anyway. The new addition was totally paid for shortly after its completion.

We have so much to praise God for!

I n 1982, Norma and I were invited to speak at Tibb Gethin's Mount Lebanon Prayer Group, one of America's longest-running prayer meetings.

The Holy Spirit told us to share how the Lord had delivered both of us from the spirit of poverty.

Financial Miracles Work Both Ways

On the way back to the station, I was pondering the fact that we had experienced a wonderful anointing of the Holy Spirit at the prayer meeting. The Lord promptly told me to write the story to be published as a book.

About that time we were invited to minister in Europe for several weeks. I thought of writing in my spare time during both flights and while in Europe, but I wasn't at all prepared for what happened.

I couldn't sleep a wink on the planes from Pittsburgh to New York to Frankfort. I wrote all night.

I couldn't sleep in Europe either, so most nights I wrote until daybreak. During the day, however, I was so sleepy I could hardly preach.

At one service the man sitting beside me on the platform nudged me with his elbow and said, "He's introducing you." I had been sound asleep, sitting up!

"I am going to sleep on the plane going home!" I said determinedly, but I was still wide awake. As a result, *Learning to Know God As Provider* was completed in the rough by the time we arrived home in Pittsburgh. I have never had insomnia like that at any other time in my life.

With 50,000 copies in print, the book has gone across the English-speaking world, blessing Christians who have had financial problems. For a number of years we sent a free copy of this book to all new donors.

I perceive our ministry to be highly focused on four areas of human need: salvation, baptism in the Holy Spirit, healing and health, and freedom from poverty. All these subjects demand anointed teaching on television. The four areas of need have developed out of my study of the Bible during more than 40 years.

Telethons provide grand opportunities to teach viewers about how to be delivered from the spirit of poverty.

Mike Murdock, R.W. Schambach, Richard Roberts, and a number of other greatly anointed teachers have been mightily used by God. They have started countless Christians on the path to financial freedom by the simple, yet widely misunderstood and criticized, biblical principle of sowing seed for prosperity (based upon Luke 6:38, 2 Corinthians 9:6-13, and other scriptures).

Mike Murdock ministering on Cornerstone TeleVision.

I am totally convinced that Jesus wants His people freed from poverty. Those who believe this truth genuinely experience the peace and joy that come with deliverance from the ugly spirit of poverty. Ironically, countless wealthy people are still tormented daily by this demon.

Financial Miracles Work Both Ways

Norma and I both have learned from personal experience the *practical* side of this blessed biblical teaching of planting financial seed for a financial harvest. After all, the Lord Jesus has a lot of work to be accomplished by His Church in preparation for His soon Return, and some of that work is expensive. He is depending upon the Body of Christ to finance His end-time harvest of souls.

I hate poverty! Having grown up with it, I know that awful feeling in the pit of my stomach. I can still recall those lonely, desperate times of worry about money.

With Norma's help I learned that poverty is a *spiritual* problem. In Second Corinthians 9:6-13, God tells us how to be set free from that evil spirit. Norma and I were both delivered from that ugly demon while I was on a very limited salary.

I love to hear or read the testimony of a Christian who has been set free from this spirit of poverty—especially because it happened to both Norma and me—and particularly when it happens through the ministry of Cornerstone TeleVision.

Planting financial seed for a harvest truly works.

Tim Horton, our former station manager in Schenectady, New York, has a son, Marcus, who had been born autistic. Marcus was three years old, had never spoken a word, and would allow no one to touch him except his mother. Tim was brokenhearted. Whenever he would lovingly touch his son, the boy would scream and fight viciously.

During a telethon, as Mike Murdock was teaching the biblical principle of sowing and reaping, Tim and his wife pledged $1,000 as a seed for Marcus' deliverance from autism. Spectacularly, within days Marcus began to speak a few words.

When Tim came home from work, Marcus would run to him, jumping in his dad's arms. Some weeks later Marcus had a vocabulary of about 70 words, and he continued to improve. Later they realized that Marcus was an unusually bright child.

All these blessings started with a $1,000 seed and the touch of a faithful God.

S atan's primary attack against Christian television stations comes in his attempt to steal our finances.

In all these years we probably have not had enough money to pay all our bills for more than several months—all together. As a result, we must plan and pray a great deal concerning our fund-raising. Telethons are both hard work and lots of fun.

Some viewers love to watch telethons; others say they hate them. I think I know why.

The Holy Spirit brings conviction of sin in people's hearts, and conviction feels bad (John 16:8). That's why most unbelievers hate to hear the gospel preached. Thus, those who don't like telethons—even Christians—are actually under conviction to contribute liberally, so they feel quite uncomfortable in their hearts. It's not the fund-raising that offends; it's the supernatural work of the Spirit!

One telethon evening, Mike Murdock began to talk to the viewers—not about pledges, but about eternal life. Within several hours more than 250 phoned to accept Jesus or to rededicate their lives to Him. We didn't raise a lot of money that evening, but the next day we were blessed with more pledges than any other day in that telethon. God honored the first night's salvation appeal!

I n recent years, the telethons have become even more exciting for me as I'm able to put my love of maps into action. Nothing thrills me more than to read pledges from distant states (we've had gifts from all 50 states, including

Financial Miracles Work Both Ways

Hawaii and Alaska)—and foreign countries, including all the Canadian provinces from Newfoundland to British Columbia, along with Mexico, Bermuda, Jamaica, the Bahamas, Barbados, Trinidad, and many other Caribbean nations!

My favorite pledges from that area of the world come from Montserrat. During the eruption of the Soufrière Hills, the British government made provision for all the citizens to evacuate the island. Some folks, however, stubbornly remained in their homes.

We were having a telethon at the time and received pledges from viewers living in the very shadow of that angry volcano. One pastor who faithfully remained with his little church flock phoned from Montserrat to ask Evelyn Kean what health products she could suggest for the smoky atmosphere there. We took a few moments to pray for those courageous Christians.

Still further south, we have also received pledges from South American countries, including Colombia, Venezuela, and French Guiana. Amazing!

We normally give each telethon a title. The favorite title is *Faith Works!* And we've discovered that, indeed, *faith works!*

E very once in a while, for some unknown reason, a telethon will go "flat." We pray, we work hard, yet little happens: Few people are saved, pledges drop off sharply, and an unusual heaviness settles upon the studio. The viewers can feel it, too. We always ask God for His anointing, but on these rare occasions, it just isn't there.

One of those strange experiences occurred in the autumn of 1994. In spite of the struggle, the Lord came through. During the telethon, He provided the largest bequest we've ever received—$284,000—and we made our goal! He's a faithful God!

Telethons generate a lot of excitement. A viewer called me during a telethon with this thrilling challenge: "I will match every amount contributed during a 30-minute period—with no limit!"

Now *that* was an exciting challenge! I recall it was on a Thursday evening.

The previous Sunday morning, a Christian businessman had told his wife in church, "I think we should give Cornerstone TeleVision the $50,000 that I set aside."

His wife disagreed and became very angry. In the middle of the church service, the two of them had a heated argument. The husband was so irritated that he walked home from church, refusing to ride in the car with his wife.

For several days, the husband fumed. Suddenly the Lord spoke to his wife and told her to give Cornerstone the $50,000.

The businessman immediately phoned the station, asking to speak to me. His call came right in the middle of the matching challenge on that same Thursday evening. Within an hour, he drove to the station and handed me the money.

God's timing was exquisite! It reminded me of God's timing of the landslide that dammed up the Jordan River precisely as the Israelites were starting across into the Promised Land (see Joshua 3).

Instead of matching $28,000, the donor who had made the challenge had to match $78,000! The partner swallowed hard but was quite honorable about it.

This generous donor told me on the phone, "I'm retired, and I'm giving out of my principal; but I feel strongly that it's better to give while you're alive to see it work for the Kingdom than after you're dead."

Financial Miracles Work Both Ways

That advice leads to a story Pat Robertson related to me many years ago. A missionary-statesman told Pat he was praying one day and asked the Lord, "Why don't Christians give more money for foreign missions since the need is so great?"

Suddenly he had a vision. The Lord showed him a large table, with money, stocks, bonds, certificates of deposit—all piled high on the table. The Spirit then spoke to him: "That's money owned by Christians; take all you want."

As the missionary reached out to pick up some of the money, a big, hairy arm—the arm of the Antichrist—elbowed its way in front of him and scooped *all* the money off the table. *"That,"* said the Spirit of God, "is what's going to happen to the money Christians have been keeping for themselves!"

I am convinced that was a true vision from God.

Two of our favorite people are Charles and Frances Hunter. Both of them continue to serve the Lord aggressively in spite of their advanced ages. Although widely criticized by some Christians, Charles and Frances have personally led more people into the Kingdom than *any* of their critics.

Isn't is amazing that most of the truly effective evangelists are so bitterly criticized by other Christians!

I am reminded of a pastor's complaint to evangelist D.L. Moody: "I don't like your offensive method of evangelism!"

Moody responded humbly, "I don't like it either. How do *you* do evangelism?"

"Well...I don't know that I do any evangelism."

"In that case," responded Moody, "I like my offensive method better than your method of none at all!"

The Hunters, too, persist in their unique ministry, gently forgiving the undeserved attacks that come their way. Humility is one of the Hunters' distinctive qualities; they'd rather brag on Jesus!

They have given literally every significant amount of their personal wealth to the Lord.

During the 1970's, when Norma and I first told the Hunters about the vision for a television station, Charles responded immediately: "The Lord told me just this morning that someone would ask us for financial help today, and we were to give that person some money."

Charles immediately wrote a check for $1,000, and they have continued to contribute through the years—in spite of the fact that they cannot receive Cornerstone's signal where they live.

We try to schedule the Hunters as often as possible.

Their very *first* Healing Explosion was held in Pittsburgh's Civic Arena. For five evenings before the healing service at the Arena, Charles and Frances taught on WPCB-TV.

The night of the Healing Explosion, the Arena management estimated the audience at 10,500—one of the Hunters' largest services ever in this country. The miracles were spectacular!

After the Arena service, Norma was approached by an excited elderly couple: "I can think!" he screamed. "I can think!"

When Norma looked puzzled, his wife exploded with joy: "He's had Alzheimer's, and now his mind is clear! Oh, praise the Lord!"

Charles and Frances Hunter at Pittsburgh's Civic Arena with more than 10,000 needy people.

Hundreds of blessed testimonies resulted from that initial Healing Explosion. That event inaugurated the Hunters' large Healing Explosions around the world, in which ordinary believers themselves are trained to heal the sick.

Frances goes so hard for Jesus that she has literally burned herself out. Without the power of the Holy Spirit, a number of her illnesses would have killed her. But God has been faithful, and she has been restored from almost all those physical problems.

Frances often says she has more new parts than originals. On her 80th birthday, I faxed Frances a birthday greeting, noting some of the new body parts that God has given her through the years:

Norma and I were rolling on the floor with laughter when we heard that you were going to be 80 years old. We just don't believe it!

263

After all, your heart isn't over 25 years old, your thyroid and your pancreas are younger than that. You have two brand-new hips, and your immune system is younger still. So how much of Frances are we congratulating on her 80th birthday?

The Hunters' secretary told me that the staff posted my fax for several weeks and read it whenever they wanted a laugh. Frances tells us that she has read that letter in services across the world, using it as a faith builder for their audiences.

After the Hunters were at Cornerstone for a three-day Summer Celebration, we received some highly critical calls and letters. The incredible evidence of joy in the studio prompted some viewers to call our behavior "disgusting."

For example, an attractive blonde woman lay on the studio floor for nearly an hour—laughing and rolling from side to side like a "holy roller." This offended some viewers, but they didn't hear the explanation I heard.

When this woman—still laughing quite loudly—was finally lifted to her feet, she tried to explain the reason for her great joy.

"Russ," she blurted out between peals of laughter, "my father molested me when I was three..."—more laughter—"and I watched him murder my brother!" She sounded as if this were the funniest story she had ever told.

Two of her friends had to help her—still laughing—out the door.

What was going on with this woman? Jesus was merely doing what He did when He walked the hills of Galilee. The Spirit of Jesus was granting her "deliverance"; she was being delivered from years of horrible emotional pain.

Like the Pharisees of Jesus' day, many still criticize His work as they did 2,000 years ago. Pharisees were—and

Charles and Frances Hunter ministering in the joy of the Lord.

still are—people who love God but who refuse to let Him do things *His* way.

John Calvin, a genuine sourpuss, was a bachelor and a lawyer by training, who lived in Geneva, Switzerland, during the sixteenth century. Calvin and his followers founded the "Reformed" group of churches, including Presbyterian, United Church of Christ, Reformed, and Congregational churches.

The Calvinists brought "iron" into the blood of American Protestantism and set the stage for the American Constitution. Their Puritanism, however, squelched the joy that is very much a part of New Testament Christianity. Jesus is now restoring that joy to His Church—at least to those who will receive it.

The "joy of the Lord" is an important theological matter. In fact, it's found a number of times in the New Testament and is always a sure sign of the Holy Spirit's presence. Joy is an assurance from God.

Second, the joy of the Lord brings *healing*. Every Christian knows that "a merry heart doeth good like a medicine" (Proverbs 17:22a KJV).

Third, the joy of the Lord brings deliverance from demonic oppression, as we have already seen in some anecdotes shared earlier. "Holy laughter" is quite scriptural.

Finally, the joy of the Lord is God's preparation and provision for persecution of the Lord's people. In a real sense, He is "arming" His Church to help sustain us through the difficult times ahead.

I n order to understand the nature of the divine healings that are needed, Charles and Frances Hunter have made quite a study of the human body.

Charles says, "Prayer for healing is much more effective if the person doing the ministry knows exactly what the correct diagnosis is. Then he can speak to the specific condition." Their extensive record of healings spectacularly verifies this method. In fact, the Hunters' rate of healing carpal tunnel syndrome approaches 100 percent!

More than 6,000 copies of their 52-hour-long videotape training courses on healing are evangelizing significant areas of Russia and the Ukraine. When Russian-language healing videotapes are shown in a home, people are consistently healed on the spot. As a result, a Christian church will often be organized right in that Russian home, many of the members newly born again.

Charles and Frances both have a great sensitivity to the voice of the Spirit—and they believe Him with childlike faith.

In 1991, Charles reported to me, "God told me we are to 'take a census of the world'!"

Financial Miracles Work Both Ways

Such a massive undertaking sounded rather presumptuous. After all, lots of other international ministries are already going door-to-door, proclaiming the gospel. I even wondered to myself, "Is Charles getting too old to hear the Lord's voice accurately?"

Charles and Frances' excitement usually overwhelms any opposition, and I soon offered to inaugurate the entire affair on our new satellite hook-up.

On Sunday afternoon and evening, September 20, 1992, we went *live* across the nation as Trinity Broadcasting Network in California joined with us. Charles and Frances' "Soul-a-thon" enjoyed a sputtering start, but it was a beginning.

Slowly a few Third World countries began participating. The first notable success came from Honduras, where almost two million persons—more than one-third of the entire population of that Central American nation—committed their lives to Jesus Christ! It literally changed that nation. I'm sure that revival helped greatly during and following the 1998 flooding.

Since then, a number of other nations have also had similar thrilling censuses, including Ghana, Nicaragua, Peru, portions of India, and especially, the Philippines.

Many *tens of millions* of additional people worldwide will be in heaven because of one man's (with Frances' excited support) childlike trust in an unlikely word from God. By December 31, 1998, the total of those committing their lives to Jesus through this worldwide census had reached 100 million!

If every born-again Christian in the world shared the Hunters' enthusiasm for Jesus, He'd probably return before the end of this very year.

Chapter 16

The Sky's the Limit!

The April 1991 telethon was a most unusual and historic experience. The predetermined goal had almost been reached with one evening to go! That had never occurred before.

"What should we do on this final Friday evening?" we asked one another.

All our executives were meeting in Oleen's office when she mentioned, "My husband Ted has located an almost-new satellite earth station for sale for $250,000."

"Really?"

"It would have cost over a million dollars originally," she noted.

"We can't afford to *rent* space on a satellite, let alone purchase that massive earth station," Oleen continued, and we all agreed. Still, the opportunity intrigued us.

As we discussed the pros and cons, I played "the devil's advocate," deliberately trying to find reasons why we shouldn't do it.

Still, the others defended—seemingly irrationally—proceeding with such a project.

Even our very conservative Oleen started giving reasons why we should buy it. "I can't believe I'm saying this!" exclaimed Oleen again and again.

Then we came upon a solution. Why not let *the Lord* decide?

"What's the most we've ever received in one evening of telethon?" someone asked.

"$64,000," was the reply. "Just last Monday."

"If God gives us pledges totaling an impossible $250,000 this evening," I proposed, "then we'll know we're to purchase the earth station."

Since God specializes in the impossible, that seemed just fine with all of us.

"So, Lord, *You* tell us while we're on the air!" we prayed.

At any rate, He hadn't spoken to me personally—as He had promised to do concerning any major decision. Perhaps He wanted to speak to all of us at the same time!

We went on the air at 7:00 p.m., explaining that we were considering purchasing a satellite earth station. Before we finished describing the project, the first pledge came in—$1,000— followed immediately by one for $25,000! That second caller said, "I've got to put this money in the mail before I get scared! But I know I heard from God!"

Other pledges followed immediately: $1,000! $2,000! $1,000! $1,000!

A pastor who was watching with a friend, told her, "I'm supposed to give $5,000 for that project, and so are *you*!" Together they provided another $10,000!

The Sky's the Limit!

Although the entire evening was relatively subdued—the quietest telethon event we've ever known—the power of God was poured out at a magnitude we'd never seen. Nearly everyone in the studio was in tears as a holy awe affected us all.

A lady wrote to tell how she always tried to give to Cornerstone TeleVision without her husband's finding out. Once, when her husband learned of her gift, he exploded: "What's the matter with you? You know they're just a bunch of thieves!"

That evening she was watching and wishing she could pledge $200 for the satellite uplink, but her husband was in the house. Just then she felt him standing behind her chair, watching the telethon over her head. While she was waiting for the usual nasty wisecrack, he asked, "You'd like to give to that, wouldn't you?"

His wife answered uneasily, "Uh...yes."

"I think we should give $1,000!"

She nearly fell off her chair in amazement.

Other people described how they felt the Holy Spirit "sucking" them right into their television screens—almost like some of the silly commercials we see nowadays. The power was so intense.

One couple had gotten undressed to go to bed but redressed quickly and rushed to the studio to experience the power in person.

Pastor Al Rowan had just returned from an all-day bus tour with senior citizens from his church when he turned on the telethon. Suddenly he told his wife Linda, "I've got to get over there!"

He walked into the studio and onto the set, still wearing a leather jacket. Al gave an anointed prophecy that resulted in waves of $1,000 pledges.

From left to right: Dr. Mitchel Nickols, Ron Hembree, Norma, Russ, and Pastor Al Rowan praising the Lord for the miracle of $250,000 for the satellite uplink, April 19, 1991.

At precisely 12:45 a.m. a final $1,000 pledge was phoned in, making the total exactly $250,000! *Four* times more than any amount ever pledged before!

God had spoken—loud and clear. We were to go on satellite! He was moving us up—once again telling us to fulfill one great mission more than we could afford.

We purchased the enormous satellite dish and all that went with that huge earth station. Several large trucks were required to haul it from Illinois, and we had no money for the shipping costs.

Each day, we shared the progress of the satellite project during *Getting Together*—and the needed funds came in steadily.

Satellite earth station being erected.

Engineers dwarfed beneath the huge satellite dish.

Rocket at Cape Canaveral being readied to launch Cornerstone's first satellite.

The Sky's the Limit!

Although the dismantling and reassembling of the equipment were also expensive, we were able to tell the viewers—for the first and only time in Cornerstone's history: "Enough! The satellite earth station and its installation are totally paid for!"

Oleen had prayed for years that some day we'd be able to say, "Enough!"

Our engineers loved the challenge and did very well assembling and testing the satellite.

On June 4, 1992, the new ground station sent our signal skyward to the satellite 23,000 miles above the Equator.

At the time, however, we *still* didn't have enough money for the first month's rent. God's timing once again proved to be perfect. That month happened to be one of those rare times when a surplus of satellite channels was available! We were able to lease a satellite channel for far less than the usual cost.

When Oleen negotiated the contract with the satellite company, she was operating in totally unfamiliar territory. She asked the Lord for wisdom, and He gave her some seemingly trivial details to add to the contract. These "details" later turned out to give Cornerstone great financial advantages, and we are still benefiting from the residual effects of that "bargain" blessing.

In the early years, we were consistently late with our monthly payments, but sooner or later we made them all. Today the satellite payments total more than $1,000,000 each year. And WPCB-TV is still to this day "Superstation WPCB-TV"!

On Monday evening, just prior to that memorable Friday, April 19, 1991, our staff gathered in prayer before going on the air for the telethon. Suddenly, the Lord spoke to me: "Tell them, as I told ancient Israel..."

Comfort, comfort my people, says your God. Speak tenderly to Jerusalem, and cry to her that her warfare is ended, that her suffering is accepted... (Isaiah 40:1-2, paraphrased).

I shared that message from the Lord with excitement. I just knew that our telethons would be different from that day forward. Indeed, that Monday evening God set the record of $64,000—a record destined to fall only four days later with that miraculous total of $250,000.

Ever since that prophetic word, the telethons have rarely dragged, but rather are quite inspirational, exciting, and productive, empowering Cornerstone's dramatic Spirit-led growth.

Another opportunity came our way with a phone call from Pastor David Wells of Schenectady, New York.

"You have been recommended to me because of your integrity," David told me. "Years ago, I leased a television station in our area, but all the cable systems refused to carry our Christian signal. As a result, the ministry has gone bankrupt. The owner worked his way through several other operators, none of whom could make it financially."

I was getting excited!

"Now," David continued, "the owner is willing to sell the station for $375,000, and he's looking to me to make a recommendation. Are you interested?"

"I sure am!"

We borrowed the money from our bank and went to examine WOCD-TV, Channel 55. The transmitter/tower were located in Amsterdam, New York, and the studio and offices were in Scotia, just north of Schenectady.

The Sky's the Limit!

We knew that Channel 55 was worth far more than we had paid for it, but our engineers found that it had been terribly abused by incompetent engineers. Parts of the transmitter and associated equipment needed to be rebuilt—a job requiring many months of labor. Even after the repairs, the transmitter would simply shut down inexplicably.

On one of those occasions Blake Richert, our Vice President for Engineering, told the other two engineers, "We've got to lay our hands on this transmitter and pray!"

Our on-site engineer, Tom, had never heard of such a thing, but he went along with it.

After leading in prayer, Blake said, "I know now. The trouble's right here. We've got to take this thing apart."

"But we've already checked that."

"I don't care," insisted Blake. "The problem's in here. We prayed, and I know it!" And it was. Now *that's* the faith Christian television engineers need! The on-site engineer was shocked! Few engineers are accustomed to miracles.

Meanwhile, Congress passed a new law mandating that cable systems were to carry all the full-power television stations in their markets. We immediately notified all the cable companies in the Albany-Schenectady-Troy area. A number of the smaller systems—knowing we couldn't afford to sue them all—simply refused to obey the law. The manager of the Albany system (the largest) was adamant.

The FCC moved so slowly that it took a year and a half before they ordered the Albany cable specifically to carry WOCD-TV, Channel 55. Even then, the Albany cable company did not add us to their entire system, nor did they include us in their primary tier. Our legal costs to make them comply were astronomical.

After several years, we decided that we couldn't hold on any longer. Only half the money needed to operate Channel 55 was coming from that viewing area, and the financial burden was threatening to destroy our entire ministry. Reluctantly, we realized that WOCD-TV had to be sold.

Norma cutting the ribbon to inaugurate the new WOCD-TV, Channel 55 in Schenectady, New York. Seated from left to right: Russ, Norma, Ron Hembree, Mrs. Wells and Pastor David Wells. Standing: Tim Horton (with beard) and local pastors and their wives.

WOCD-TV, which had been dedicated to the Lord from the beginning, needed a buyer who would let us have some time to present Christian programing. We began to pray.

When Bud Paxson of Paxson Communications offered to let us have three hours daily—plus the Worship Channel all night—we turned down another offer and several million dollars in profit.

Although Paxson Communications paid us no more than we had invested in it, at least I could sleep peacefully, knowing that the Capital Region of New York was receiving as much Christian television as possible.

Many years ago I met Bob Johnson, who told me about a future technology for satellite distribution of television signals. Called Direct Broadcast Satellite, it requires only a small, 18-inch dish, which may be attached outside a window or on a roof.

"It will replace the large five- to ten-foot dishes some day," Bob told me.

From time to time I heard about Bob, who had set up shop in Naples, Florida. I really didn't think much about DBS, since we were already over our heads in monthly rent on the C-band satellite.

In the autumn of 1995, the Spirit of God told me to call Bob Johnson. No other instructions; just call.

I thought I would tell him about the great programs we were producing, and perhaps he would put several of them on his future Direct Broadcast Satellite.

Bob was available, and I introduced myself: "Do you remember meeting me on such-and-such an occasion?"

"No, we've never met."

"Aren't you the Bob Johnson I met in 1978?" And I named the place.

"No, I am sometimes confused with that Bob Johnson."

"Well, I'm sorry. I guess I have the wrong man." And I wondered why God had me call the wrong person.

"Actually, you didn't make a mistake," Bob responded. "I've heard about you, Russ, and I was going to call *you* next week. I understand you are producing some good Christian programs. We'd be interested in looking at them."

One thing led to another, and soon Oleen and Blake flew to Florida. They came to an agreement with Bob Johnson of Dominion Foundation that he would carry certain of our programs on his future DBS satellite.

Bob showed Oleen a list of all the national programs he wanted to carry in addition to ours, and that gave Oleen a bright idea: "Bob, we already carry every one of those programs on our C-band satellite feed. Why don't you just take our entire lineup, and then you won't need to be skipping around? You can leave your receiver on that one satellite."

Bob was enthusiastic. And so, although the rent on the C-band satellite costs us more than $1,000,000 a year, the Direct Broadcast Satellite is totally *free*! God worked *another* financial miracle!

We're currently on EchoStar III, "The Dish Network," *Sky Angel* Channel 673.

WPCB-TV is now a superstation *twice*!

A lso during autumn 1995, the Spirit of God told me to contact the Chief Executive Officer at WQED Pittsburgh, the company that controlled the two local PBS television stations.

"Offer to buy their second station—WQEX, Channel 16," He instructed. "Then sell Channel 40."

The Sky's the Limit!

Channel 40 is a *commercial* allocation while Channel 16 is *noncommercial*; thus our Channel 40 was worth much, much more in the marketplace.

We entered into agreements with WQED Pittsburgh and Paxson Communications that provide for Cornerstone to move from Channel 40 to Channel 16 and for Paxson to acquire Channel 40. The agreements are subject to approval of the FCC. As this book is going to press in February 1999, we are still waiting for the Commission to grant its approval of the channel exchange.

Visitors (especially those involved in television) cannot believe that we do so much with so little. God miraculously stretches our money, and we have a very talented, dedicated staff. By any standard of measure, Cornerstone TeleVision has been blessed by God.

With no outstanding on-air personality and without cash resources, a tiny, barely alive ministry has risen to international prominence over the past 20 years by the grace of God. Some ministry leaders who belong to the National Religious Broadcasters seem to perceive Cornerstone as an ideal to emulate. Even the radio ministries with a dispensationalist orientation appear pleased to be associated with Cornerstone.

I see eight reasons for God's blessing upon this ministry:

1. God's calling. We know that we have been chosen to do Christian television.

2. Our trust in the supernatural power of the Holy Spirit.

3. Integrity, honesty, and forthrightness. These are expensive qualities to maintain in the short run, but they are blessed of God over the long haul.

4. Our love for the viewers who are hurting, and especially our appreciation for those who support Cornerstone TeleVision financially.

5. None of us who are executives load up on "perks"; we don't take advantage of our positions. We have a genuine fear of God.

6. Our continuing, careful commitment to tithe all contributions. (This one is so vital, but I can't persuade most of my colleagues around the nation to tithe from their ministries!)

7. Our respect and concern for other Christian television ministries.

8. Forgiveness for those who have attacked or injured us. Sometimes the problem is no more than a simple misunderstanding.

I have always been convinced that the Lord will honor such a style of ministry because these commitments emulate His own personality.

I've often felt like a strange choice. Why would the Lord select me to head up a major television ministry? I am neither a good businessman nor a decisive manager—not even a hard driver like so many great leaders.

Shy and reserved, I'm not at all the type of personality you'd expect to see on television. My voice is soft, almost "fuzzy," and not a clear speaking voice.

The Sky's the Limit!

Having made so many mistakes in building this ministry, I cannot imagine another human who would select Russ Bixler to be the Chairman and Chief Executive Officer of a nation-wide television ministry.

"But," as the apostle Paul said in First Corinthians 15:10, "by the grace of God I am what I am"—what He's called me to be—and I trust Him with my life. I identify further with the apostle as he noted, "...[God] had set me apart before I was born..." (Galatians 1:15). I can never forget that sense of divine election.

I have always thought that God had chosen me for Christian television because I am so ecumenical, and further, that I can believe Him for the impossible. I also know that He wouldn't have used me if I hadn't forgiven those who came against me.

May 1998, however, held a great surprise. I had just finished telling on the air of an event that had happened one Christmas long ago, before 1970.

During the 1960's, when I was pastor of the Pittsburgh Church of the Brethren, Norma and I used to have an "open house" in the parsonage for the members of our congregation after the morning service on the Sunday before Christmas. We had recently been baptized in the Holy Spirit, and we were just learning how to walk in the Spirit.

Norma needed about $80 worth of groceries for the occasion, but we had only $36 in our checking account. My next paycheck wouldn't come until after Christmas, and I had no idea where we'd get the additional $44. We had no savings and always lived from payday to payday.

I didn't tell Norma; I was too ashamed. I just prayed. About a day before we had to purchase the groceries, I was sitting at my desk, opening the day's mail.

The first letter was a request from a missionary program. Well, we couldn't give, so it went into the wastebasket. The next letter was asking for a contribution, too. As I threw it into the wastebasket, that familiar quiet Voice spoke: "Take those two letters out of the wastebasket and give them each a gift."

"But, Lord! I don't have enough money now!"

"I know it," came the soft reply.

"But, Lord! I don't have enough money!"

"I know it."

That precious Voice had never misled me. Was this to be the first time? Reluctantly, I hurried next door to the parsonage, quietly getting the checkbook without saying anything to Norma.

There was the $36. "I'll give each ministry $10."

"No!" the Voice became forceful. "I want it all!"

"But, Lord, I don't have enough money now!"

"I know it."

So, with sweating hands I wrote two $18 checks, leaving just a few cents to keep the checking account open. I hurriedly put stamps on them and rushed to the mailbox before my "good judgment" could take over.

As I returned to my study, I felt like a "suffering servant of God," so I turned to that passage in the Bible for comfort. The "Suffering Servant" narrative begins at Isaiah 52:13: "Behold, my servant shall prosper...."

Those five words actually lifted off the page for a couple of seconds, "Behold, my servant shall prosper...," and then retreated to the Bible. I watched it happen.

I stared at that sentence, fascinated, and then began to laugh. I laughed and laughed, totally forgetting about my financial predicament. I was so free that I returned to work on my Christmas sermon in peace.

Within an hour the door opened, and an Episcopalian friend walked in. "Merry Christmas, Russ! The Lord just told me to give this to you!" He threw a check on my desk and walked out. It was $100!

Ever since, Norma and I have been convinced of the scriptural principle of sowing seed for a financial harvest. Luke 6:38 came to life for us that day!

Thirty years later I told this story on television. Many viewers were blessed—and also learned a valuable lesson.

A few moments later the Spirit spoke in my heart, "That's why I chose you for Christian television!"

I almost cried.

My instant obedience was apparently the key for the Lord. That possibility had never occurred to me before. What a delightful surprise!

Occasionally God speaks to me about a major matter, and I have the simple faith to believe that He will accomplish what He declares—no matter what the obstacles are.

Meanwhile, we have a continent—even a world—to win for Jesus before He returns. Thank God for the tens of thousands of viewers who share that vision with us!

And I know one more great truth: Cornerstone TeleVision is to be a herald of the soon-coming of the Lord!

So much more could be recounted, but where do I stop? The stories, the miracles, the salvations, the joy, the tears—they go on and on.

Perhaps we should end this blessed 30-year (1969–1999) testimony of God's goodness as the apostle John ended his testimony following the three greatest years of human history:

But there are also many other things which Jesus did; were every one of them to be written, I suppose that the world itself could not contain the books that would be written (John 21:25).

For two decades Cornerstone TeleVision has been ministering to millions through a powerful combination of top quality, award-winning programs and a genuine concern for the prayer needs of the audience.

Across these 20 years...
- Thousands of viewers have phoned or written to say they've come to Christ as a direct result of the broadcasts.
- More than 1.1 million viewers have called the prayer line for spiritual support.
- Some 17,000-plus people have called to report that God has answered their prayers directly through Cornerstone TeleVision.

Today Cornerstone TeleVision, Inc., includes WPCB-TV, Channel 40 of Pittsburgh; WKBS-TV, Channel 47 of Altoona, Pennsylvania; W50BF of Hermitage/Sharon, Pennsylvania; and 24-hour nationwide satellite signals on Space Net 4, Channel 19, and Sky Angel, Channel 673. Broadcasting from Pittsburgh, Pennsylvania, Cornerstone TeleVision now covers most of North and Central America and the Caribbean.

For more information on Cornerstone TeleVision and its ministry, contact:

Cornerstone TeleVision, Inc.
Signal Hill Drive
Wall, PA 15148-1499

(412) 824-3930 (Business Office)
(412) 824-3900 (Prayer Line)
Website: www.ctv.org

Other exciting titles by R. Russell Bixler

EARTH, FIRE, AND SEA

by R. Russell Bixler.

Do biblical creationism and modern-day science go together? In *Earth, Fire, and Sea* Russ Bixler takes a fresh look at the biblical account of creation and provides some surprising insights into these issues. As a former pastor and now head of a Christian television company, Russ Bixler is an avid student of God's Word and of His truth. Here he challenges both current creationism and modern science to reexamine their disciplines in the light of these conclusions.

ISBN 1-56043-342-6 $12.99p

Available at your local Christian bookstore.
Internet: http://www.reapernet.com

Prices subject to change without notice.

Other
Destiny Image **titles**
you will enjoy reading

DIGGING THE WELLS OF REVIVAL
by Lou Engle.
Did you know that just beneath your feet are deep wells of revival? God is calling us today to unstop the wells and reclaim the spiritual inheritance of our nation, declares Lou Engle. As part of the pastoral staff at Harvest Rock Church and founder of its "24-Hour House of Prayer," he has experienced firsthand the importance of knowing and praying over our spiritual heritage. Let's renew covenant with God, reclaim our glorious roots, and believe for the greatest revival the world has ever known!
ISBN 0-7684-2015-6 $10.99p

ANOINTED OR ANNOYING?
by Ken Gott.
Don't miss out on the powerful move of God that is in the earth today! When you encounter God's Presence in revival, you have a choice—accept it or reject it; become anointed or annoying! Ken Gott, former pastor of Sunderland Christian Centre and now head of Revival Now! International Ministries, calls you to examine your own heart and motives for pursuing God's anointing, and challenges you to walk a life of obedience!
ISBN 0-7684-1003-7 $10.99p

THE HIDDEN POWER OF PRAYER AND FASTING
by Mahesh Chavda.
How do you react when overwhelming defeat stares you in the eye? What do you do when faced with insurmountable odds? God has provided a way to turn certain defeat into awesome victory—through prayer and fasting! An international evangelist and the senior pastor of All Nations Church in Charlotte, North Carolina, Mahesh Chavda has seen firsthand the power of God released through a lifestyle of prayer and fasting. Here he shares from decades of personal experience and scriptural study principles and practical tips about fasting and praying. This book will inspire you to tap into God's power and change your life, your city, and your nation!
ISBN 0-7684-2017-2 $10.99p

WHEN GOD STRIKES THE MATCH
by Dr. Harvey R. Brown, Jr.
A noted preacher, college administrator, and father of an "all-American" family— what more could a man want? But when God struck the match that set Harvey Brown ablaze, it ignited a passion for holiness and renewal in his heart that led him into a head-on encounter with the consuming fire of God.
ISBN 0-7684-1000-2 $11.99p

Available at your local Christian bookstore.

Internet: http://www.reapernet.com

Other *Destiny Image titles* you will enjoy reading

ENCOUNTERING THE PRESENCE
by Colin Urquhart.
What is it about Jesus that, when we encounter Him, we are changed? When we encounter the Presence, we encounter the Truth, because Jesus is the Truth. Here Colin Urquhart, best-selling author and pastor in Sussex, England, explains how the Truth changes facts. Do you desire to become more like Jesus? The Truth will set you free!
ISBN 0-7684-2018-0 $10.99p

THE GOD CHASERS
by Tommy Tenney.
Are you dissatisfied with "church"? Are you looking for more? Do you yearn to touch God? You may be a *God chaser*! The passion of Tommy Tenney, evangelist and third-generation Pentecostal minister, is to "catch" God and find himself in God's manifest presence. For too long God's children have been content with crumbs. The Father is looking for those who will seek His face. This book will enflame your own desire to seek God with your whole heart and being—and to find Him.
ISBN 0-7684-2016-4 $11.99p

THE POWER OF BROKENNESS
by Don Nori.
Accepting Brokenness is a must for becoming a true vessel of the Lord, and is a stepping-stone to revival in our hearts, our homes, and our churches. Brokenness alone brings us to the wonderful revelation of how deep and great our Lord's mercy really is. Join this companion who leads us through the darkest of nights. Discover the *Power of Brokenness*.
ISBN 1-56043-178-4 $10.99p

Available at your local Christian bookstore.

Internet: http://www.reapernet.com

Prices subject to change without notice. B6:63

ther
Destiny Image titles
you will enjoy reading

CORPORATE ANOINTING
by Kelley Varner.
Just as a united front is more powerful in battle, so is the anointing when Christians come together in unity! In this classic book, senior pastor Kelley Varner of Praise Tabernacle in Richlands, North Carolina, presents a powerful teaching and revelation that will change your life! Learn how God longs to reveal the fullness of Christ in the fullness of His Body in power and glory.
ISBN 0-7684-2011-3 $10.99p

SECRETS OF THE MOST HOLY PLACE
by Don Nori.
Here is a prophetic parable you will read again and again. The winds of God are blowing, drawing you to His Life within the Veil of the Most Holy Place. There you begin to see as you experience a depth of relationship your heart has yearned for. This book is a living, dynamic experience with God!
ISBN 1-56043-076-1 $10.99p

THE LOST ART OF INTERCESSION
by Jim W. Goll.
The founder of Ministry to the Nations, Jim Goll has traveled the world in a teaching and prophetic ministry. All over the globe God is moving—He is responding to the prayers of His people. Here Jim Goll teaches the lessons learned by the Moravians during their 100-year prayer Watch. They sent up prayers; God sent down His power. Through Scripture, the Moravian example, and his own prayer life, Jim Goll proves that "what goes up must come down."
ISBN 1-56043-697-2 $10.99p

WORSHIP: THE PATTERN OF THINGS IN HEAVEN
by Joseph L. Garlington.
Worship and praise play a crucial role in the local church. Whether you are a pastor, worship leader, musician, or lay person, you'll find rich and anointed teaching from the Scriptures about worship! Joseph L. Garlington, Sr., a pastor, worship leader, and recording artist in his own right, shows how *worship is the pattern of things in Heaven*!
ISBN 1-56043-195-4 $10.99p

Available at your local Christian bookstore.

Internet: http://www.reapernet.com

Prices subject to change without notice.

B6:64